Also by Ken Jennings

BECAUSE I SAID SO!

The Truth Behind the Myths,
Tales, and Warnings Every Generation
Passes Down to Its Kids

Ken Jennings

Scribner
New York   London   Toronto   Sydney   New Delhi

A Division of Simon & Schuster, Inc.
1230 Avenue of the Americas
New York, NY 10020

First Scribner trade paperback edition October 2013

SCRIBNER and design are registered trademarks of The Gale Group, Inc., used under license by Simon & Schuster, Inc., the publisher of this work.

For information about special discounts for bulk purchases, please contact Simon & Schuster Special Sales at 1-866-506-1949 or business@simonandschuster.com.

The Simon & Schuster Speakers Bureau can bring authors to your live event. For more information or to book an event contact the Simon & Schuster Speakers Bureau at 1-866-248-3049 or visit our website at www.simonspeakers.com.

Designed by Carla Jayne Jones

Manufactured in the United States of America

10 9 8 7 6 5 4 3 2 1

Library of Congress Control Number: 2012027688

ISBN 978-1-4516-5625-1
ISBN 978-1-4767-0696-2 (pbk)
ISBN 978-1-4516-5627-5 (ebook)

For Dylan and Caitlin.
I hope someday you have children **just like you.**

Contents

"Don't Make Me Get the **Other** Thermometer!"
(Sickness unto Barf)

"Don't Pick at That!"
(Bumps and Bruises)

"Look Both Ways Before You Cross the Street!"
(Grievous Bodily Harm)

"You Don't Know Where That's Been!"
(Things Not to Put in Your Mouth)

"You'll Eat It and You'll Like It!"
(Mealtime Misinformation)

"Finish Your Milk!"
(And Other Drinking Problems)

"I Told You to Go Before We Left the House!"
(Bathroom Badgering)

"Your Face Will Freeze Like That!"
(Looks and Grooming)

"It's All Fun and Games Until Someone Loses an Eye!"
(Vision and Supervision)

"Don't Let the Bedbugs Bite!"
(The Science of Sleep)

"This Room Is a Pigsty!"
(Kids and Other Animals)

"Quit Eating the Paste!"
(School Days)

"Kids These Days!"
(Technology and Modern Life)

"Well, Life **Isn't** Fair!"
(The Motivational Mom)

"What If Your Friends All Jumped off a Cliff?"
(The Awkward Age)

"How Many Times Do I Have to Tell You?"
(Reader Questions)

Preface

I was sitting in my parents' kitchen not long ago when my young son, Dylan, came whipping around the corner with a grape Tootsie Pop firmly clamped in his teeth.

"Whoa, slow down!" I said. "What if you tripped and fell on your face? The lollipop stick would get jammed right through the roof of your mouth!"

Dylan's eyes got wide. "Could that *really* happen?"

I had to admit, I had no idea. This was something my mother had told me repeatedly while I was growing up, but it's not like I'd ever dug into the relevant medical literature or consulted with surgeons. What do you do when a nine-year-old calls your bluff?

"Of course it's true!" I told him. "Go sit down at the table until you're done with your lollipop." Just like with terrorists and bears! You can't show any doubt or weakness!

I found my mom and asked her to back me up: it's true about lollipop sticks and horrific puncture wounds, right? She had no idea. "That's what Grandma used to tell us," she said. "I think it also happens in a Chaim Potok novel. *The Chosen,* maybe?"

I was horrified. A fact I'd confidently passed along to my trusting children turned out to be thirdhand rumor confirmed only by a *novelist*? (A novelist-slash-rabbi, but still. And it turns out the lollipop injury isn't in *The Chosen,* anyway. It's from *In the Beginning.*) What else had I been inadvertently misleading them about? Washing behind their ears? Chewing with their mouths closed? Was our whole life together *a huge lie*?

That's the dirty secret of parenting: it's a big game of Telephone stretching back through the centuries and delivering garbled, well-intended medieval bromides to the present. Possible misinformation like the lollipop thing never gets corrected; it just goes into hibernation for a few decades and then jumps out to snare a new generation, like a seventeen-year cicada. Parents find themselves in these factual blind alleys because they have no other resource than the dimly remembered thirty-year-old lectures of their own childhoods.

Until now! In this book, I've compiled 125 of the nagging Mom- and Dad-isms that we all grew up with, and then I've meticulously researched the scientific evidence behind them. On some, I'm happy to deliver a clear-cut verdict one way or another: either confirming them as "True" or debunking them as "False." More often, though, the truth falls somewhere in between: true with an "if," false with a "but." Some of these parental clichés turn out to be accidentally right for the wrong reason (see "Eat your crusts, that's where the vitamins are!" on page 90 or "Never wake a sleepwalker!" on page 165). Others are time-tested and unimpeachably sensible . . . but still don't always hold up well in real life (see "Don't talk to strangers!" on page 57). So there are plenty of "Mostly False" and "Possibly True" verdicts in here as well.

Much of the gray area is a matter of risk assessment. Human beings, as a rule, are terrible students of probability. As a result, we develop paranoid, nightmare-inducing phobias about the unlikeliest things (plane crashes, strangers kidnapping our kids) while ignoring far more pressing risks (heart disease, car accidents). I've used the best statistics available to try to help you gauge the relative risks of different childhood activities, whether that's going outside barefoot or swallowing gum or running with scissors, but the final decision is always going to be a judgment call—like so many other elements of parenting, an art and not a science.

Take my mom's lollipop fear, for example. There is a fair bit of medical research on "pediatric oropharyngeal trauma," which is what doctors call it when kids bash up their mouths on some foreign object. A 2006 study out of Edmonton estimated that fully 1 percent of childhood injuries are oropharyngeal traumas, and another study from Pittsburgh's Children's Hospital found that puncture wounds were indeed common outcomes. Twenty-nine percent of the injuries were serious: a large laceration, or a fistula (eww) or mucosal flap (don't know what that is, but double eww). Brain damage and death are extremely rare complications, but both have happened.

So clearly I was justified in telling my son to sit down while finishing his lollipop, right? Well, maybe and maybe not. The Pittsburgh study also notes that most cases are minor and heal with no medical intervention at all, and then runs down the items that are most likely to cause this kind of trauma. Lollipops were one of the rarest culprits, causing less than 3 percent of the injuries studied and vastly outnumbered by pencils, musical instruments, toys, sticks, and so on. The hospital treated just one lollipop case every two years, on average. Meanwhile, the Tootsie Pop company alone makes twenty million lollipops *per day*. I guarantee that lots of those lollipops get eaten by kids on the go—and yet injuries are rare. So the numbers suggest that, compared to lots of other common day-to-day activities, eating-a-lollipop-not-sitting-down isn't terribly reckless. There's a fine line between making kids cautious about dangerous horseplay and just making them panicky about totally normal stuff, like moving around with a pencil or harmonica or something in their mouths.

Parents love their kids, of course, and would like to keep them safe from everything. But even if that were an achievable goal—and it's not—it might not be great in the long run for the poor kids involved. A 2009 *Time* magazine cover package on "helicopter parents" followed the first wave of hypercushioned, overparented American children into adulthood, and the results were depressing: mommy webcams in college dorms, employers like Ernst & Young preparing "parent packets" for the pushy parents of new twentysomething hires. By trying to protect our kids from every little thing, we may have created a generation of kids and young adults who don't feel confident about *anything*. So the risks need to be measured against the rewards. What if there's a 0.95 percent chance that a kid who bikes to school will get in a wreck, but a 95 percent chance that a kid who's *not* allowed to bike to school will grow up more tentative, complacent, lazy, and/or unhappy, because riding your bike to school is awesome? I feel like those percentages might not be that far off.

So I hope this book serves as a reality check for potentially jittery parents. But even if you don't have kids right now, you presumably were (or even are) one yourself. In that case, I hope this book helps inoculate you against the crazy things parents somehow still believe—and when you take away the authoritative intonation, *lots* of parental wisdom is pretty nuts. Put butter on a burn? Wear a hat if your feet are cold? Drink *eight* glasses of water a day? Is that even possible?

If you really want to know how silly much of our parental nagging sounds, ask someone from a different culture what parents harp on there. My Korean friends weren't allowed to sleep with an electric fan in their rooms, because a fan, they were told, would somehow asphyxiate them while they slept. In Russia, kids are warned not to sit on cold surfaces, or they'll freeze their gonads and wind up sterile. Germans and Czechs hear from a young age that they should never drink water after eating fruit, or they'll get a bellyache. Filipino children don't get to wear red when it's stormy, because red clothing attracts lightning. A friend's Iranian mother used to warn her against ever inhaling a cat hair. If you get one caught in your throat, she said, you'll just keep vomiting repeatedly *until you die*. I'm not poking fun at these superstitions—I just want you to realize how ridiculous our own old wives' tales would sound to someone who's never heard them before. Wait an hour after eating to swim? If you cross your eyes, they might stay that way? How, an outsider might wonder, does anyone actually believe this stuff?

And yet there are times when the oddest and the oldest bits of parental folklore turn out to be true. There are now studies showing that cold, wet feet might indeed help cause a cold and that chicken soup can fight one. Double-dipping potato chips does spread germs. Breakfast really is the most important meal of the day. Occasionally, Mom knew what she was talking about.

I've intentionally limited this book to propositions that can easily be tested scientifically, by doctors and statisticians and so forth. I've tried to back away slowly from vaguer points of parental philosophy:

minefields like homeschooling, circumcision, co-sleeping, TV banning. Anything your weird sister-in-law is always talking about on Facebook is out, basically. Sadly, I also had to avoid areas where the science is still hotly debated and inconclusive, which meant leaving out a lot of very modern parental worries: video games and social media and whatnot. In twenty years, maybe I can write a sequel in which we finally find out what was up with phthalates in plastic toys, predators on the Internet, and cell phones causing cancer. But I'm not sure how long that will take—TV is over sixty years old and experts *still* disagree on how that affects kids. So don't hold your breath. (Holding your breath for too long *is* bad for you, according to a broad scientific consensus.)

I know there's no way one book can stamp out *all* the lies parents tell their kids. You're still going to have safety lies ("The car won't run unless your seat belts are on!") and cheapskate lies ("Honey, when the ice cream man is playing music, it means his truck is all out of ice cream") and sympathy lies ("We sent your hamster to live on a farm") and keep-your-kids-out-of-therapy lies ("We love you both exactly the same!"). But the *accidental* lies should be easier to tackle. It's time to shine the cold, hard light of truth onto controversial behaviors like sitting too close to the TV, eating toothpaste, and sneezing with your eyes open.

It's not too late! Future generations will thank us.

"If You Break Your Leg, Don't Come Running to Me!"
(Spring and Summer)

"Run between the raindrops—you won't get so wet!"

Growing up in rainy Seattle, my siblings and I were often instructed to "run between the raindrops" to stay as dry as possible between the car and our errand's destination (usually some type of knitting store, if memory serves). Of course, literally running between raindrops isn't possible unless you have the slender physique of former NBA center Manute Bol and the catlike reflexes never possessed by former NBA center Manute Bol. But my mom's dictum does point to an interesting problem that has teased physicists and pedestrians alike for years: which keeps you drier in the rain, walking or running?

Consider: obviously a rain-runner will get to shelter faster than a rain-walker, but will the higher speed put him in contact with more drops as he sprints? The dilemma has been modeled mathematically several times, but there are so many variables: the speed and surface area of the walker, the angle at which the rain is falling, splashing and aerodynamic effects caused by faster movement, and so on. When Italy's Alessandro De Angelis crunched the numbers, he came out in favor of walking, but the equations of Winnipeg's Donald Craigen and British astrophysicist Nick Allen disagreed.

Luckily, this isn't a hypothetical exercise, like modeling particles in the big bang. The world is full of real raindrops and real pedestrians, so any parking lot in April can become a laboratory. When the boys on TV's *MythBusters* tried to answer the question, they got different answers each time, but viewers felt their first findings were suspect, since they used fake rain. "The Straight Dope" columnist Cecil Adams tried the experiment in 1992 (methodology: counting raindrops spattered on a piece of construction paper) and so did Thomas Peterson and Trevor Wallis, two meteorologists at the National Climatic Data Center in Asheville, North Carolina, in 1997 (methodology: weighing their clothing after their "race" to see who got wetter), and both found a clear advantage for running. In the peer-reviewed North Carolina experiment, Dr. Peterson's sweat suit absorbed seven and a half ounces of rain while he walked, 40 percent more than Dr. Wallis's did running.

Why is running the way to go? If you stand still in vertical rain, you'll only get wet on the top of your head, but once you start to move, your front starts getting wet as well. But—crucially—you don't hit fewer raindrops by moving slower! Think about it this way: in every volume of space, there's a certain density of raindrops. Your front will meet that density of drops when you get to it no matter what your speed, so going more slowly doesn't help. It turns out that real-world effects do give runners a small increase in dampness—maybe the air currents caused by running suck in more rain than they repel, or heavier footsteps cause more splashing—but that's a drop in the bucket, so to speak, compared to the wetness you'll prevent by getting to shelter quicker.

So science has finally demonstrated that people without the sense to come in out of the rain ASAP are all wet. I wonder if the National Climatic Data Center can do a peer-reviewed study on why I only have an umbrella with me when it *doesn't* rain.

TRUE.

"Stay away from the windows during a thunderstorm!"

Ah, the eternal struggle: kids who want to watch a showy lightning storm vs. the parents who want them away from the window! The

National Weather Service has your back, moms and dads: they list windows as something to avoid during a storm, in a long list that also includes other parental bugaboos like showers, sinks, light switches, and corded telephones (remember those?).

Closing the window helps, but mostly because it lowers your risk of being hit by debris—wind knocks down plenty of branches and poles during bad storms, and shards of bark and wood can fly fifty feet or more when lightning strikes a tree. Lightning can still pass through a closed window—glass is a pretty good insulator, but so is air, and lightning obviously has no problem leaping through that. But windows and doors often have metal frames and handles, which can have electrifying results for people caught opening or closing them at the wrong times.

And yet I cannot, in good conscience, top out the truth meter below at 100 percent. There are about three hundred lightning-related injuries in the U.S. every year, meaning that your odds of being hurt by lightning this year are literally one in a million. Being a window-looker-outer instead of an inner-wall-hugger during a storm will budge those odds, but only slightly. (Every few years, a lightning-strike-through-closed-window makes the news, and no doubt a few more go unreported, but it's exceedingly rare.) There are also costs to *never* getting to watch a dramatic lightning storm pass by, poetry-of-the-soul costs not easily measured by actuaries or the National Weather Service.

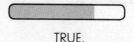

TRUE.

"Every day is Children's Day!"

Kids get to hear this one every May and June, as soon as they realize that moms and dads both get a special day for breakfast in bed and the presentation of macaroni-and-glitter handicrafts—but that no greeting cards are ever available for the other members of the family. There are certainly *many* other days of the year when adults wait on kids hand and foot (just the days that end with "y," I've found). But when kids ask, "How come there's no such thing as Children's Day?" a more accurate, less annoying answer would be, "There is! In fact, there are several."

Almost every nation on Earth celebrates a special day for children in one way or another. When I was a kid living in South Korea, it was a huge national holiday. We got May 5 off from school, making it a distinct improvement over Mother's Day and Father's Day—always Sundays, and you still have to go to church, even! In 1954, the United Nations declared every November 20 to be Universal Children's Day, a time to work for the international well-being and cooperation of children. In the United States, church observances of Children's Day actually go back to the 1850s, predating the setting aside of any specific day for mothers and fathers. Both Presidents Clinton and Bush decreed a Sunday in early June to be "National Child's Day"; President Obama moved the observance to the UN-approved November 20. Normally, there'd be grumbling in some quarters about his surrendering our sovereignty to the UN's international socialist agenda, but I'm sure we all agree that Children Are Our Future and we wouldn't want to spoil that with partisan bickering, right?

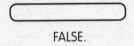

FALSE.

"No swimming for an hour after lunch—you'll cramp up!"

Perhaps no piece of dubious parental wisdom has ever been followed so precisely as this one. Stopwatches have been employed to make sure that no toe was dipped in pool water within one hour of the last bite of deviled egg or Oreo entering a child's mouth. Sixty minutes and one second: you'll be fine. Fifty-nine minutes and fifty-nine seconds: certain doom!

As early as 1961, pediatricians were doubting this old wives' tale, but it's hung on stubbornly. It is true that when we eat, our body diverts blood to the stomach to aid in digestion, but, as you may have noticed after every meal you ever ate in your life, that doesn't immediately immobilize your arms and legs. Any kind of exercise after a big meal can be uncomfortable, so I wouldn't recommend swimming the English Channel right after Thanksgiving dinner. But there's nothing magically fatal about the combination of food and chlorinated water. If you're swimming after lunch and start to feel a stitch, or bloated, or crampy, just hop out of the pool. Not one water death has ever been attributed to post-meal cramping, and the American Red Cross doesn't include any food warnings in its lengthy swimming-safety guidelines. In fact, long-distance swimmers are routinely fed in the middle of long races, to make sure they stay nourished and hydrated.

The only dangerous lunch for swimmers would be a Don Draper–style one that included a martini or two. There are about 3,500 fatal drownings in the U.S. every year, and the Centers for Disease Control says that alcohol is one of the most common factors linking them, since it can throw off a swimmer's coordination and judgment, especially in combination with sun and heat. A 1990 California study found that fully 41 percent of the state's drowning deaths were alcohol related. So listen up, moms and dads—Popsicles by the pool: fine. Peach vodka Popsicles: maybe less so.

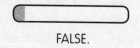

FALSE.

"Remember, there's a chemical in the pool that turns pee blue—**so we'll all know**!"

If you saw the Adam Sandler movie *Grown Ups*—well, first of all, I'm very sorry, but second, you may remember the scene in which Kevin James, swimming at a water park, reassures his daughter that the pool chemical that turns urine dark blue is "an old wives' tale." Pull back to reveal: big clouds of dark blue emanating from the trunks of *all five* of the dads! I'm laughing already!

But you should believe Kevin James's dialogue and not his sight gags. Parents have been telling their kids since at least the 1950s that *everyone will know* if they whiz in the pool, but this is a Santa-level cover-up. "You are speaking of a product that is an urban legend," a pool expert told *New York* magazine in 2010. "There is no such product available."

Anyone who took high school chemistry has used pH indicators, substances that dramatically change color in the presence of acid or alkaline substances. But these indicators won't work for urine. Your "pee-H" varies widely from acidic to alkaline depending on diet, time of day, and other factors. Urine is mostly water anyway, and the other stuff it contains (urea, salt, creatinine) is found in sweat as well, so science will probably never devise a urine indicator that's a surefire smoking, er, gun. Orson Welles told one biographer that in 1937, he and writer Charles MacArthur bought from a local chemist a colorless liquid that produced "raspberry-colored clouds" in the presence of pee, mortifying the guests at his pool parties. But given the unlikelihood of such a compound existing, we must conclude that Welles was, as impresarios are prone to do, spinning a yarn for comic effect.

The real problem with a pee detector is that busy municipal pools would probably be the urine-positive color all the time. A 2009 survey by the Water Quality and Health Council found that 17 percent of American adults admit to peeing in the pool. Imagine how high that number is for kids! Even nineteen-time gold medal winner Michael

Phelps once admitted to Jimmy Kimmel that he's been known to micturate in the natatorium.

"Which nationality pees in the pool the most?" Kimmel wanted to know.

"Probably Americans," Phelps admitted.

We're number one! We're number one!

FALSE.

"You can still get sunburned on a cloudy day, you know!"

This is often misquoted by parents and doctors as "You can get a sunburn *just as easily* on a cloudy day!" which is dead wrong. Clouds don't block all the sun's harmful ultraviolet light, just as they don't keep all the visible light from getting through, but they do dim it considerably. Even a thin, bright cloud cover will block between 15 and 40 percent of the sun's UV rays; a more overcast day will block much more.

But it's easy enough to get a painful burn from even a portion of the sun's ultraviolet output—cloud cover that blocks fully half the UV is the equivalent of wearing SPF 2 sunscreen, but the American Academy of Dermatology recommends SPF 30 at a minimum. And the cooler weather of cloudy days often fools sunbathers into staying out longer or skipping the sunblock altogether.

In fact, dermatologists say that nervous parents are right about *most* of their paranoid-sounding sun warnings. Harmful UVA rays, which can cause skin cancer and premature aging but *not* sunburn, are the part of the UV spectrum that isn't blocked by window glass, so you're still at risk in a hot car or sunny living room. It takes about an ounce—a full shot glass!—of sunscreen to protect your exposed skin, so most people don't apply enough, and they also don't reapply every two hours or after every swim as they should. It's best to put on sunscreen fifteen minutes or so before heading into the sun, because protection doesn't begin instantly. And don't believe that sunburns aren't harmful if they fade into tans rather than peeling. That's a function of the skin type you were born with, but *any* sunburn is a sign that you've damaged your skin, whether you're fair or dark or tan easily or don't.

Having just five sunburns in childhood doubles your risk of melanoma later in life. You can get the same effect from just *one* childhood sunburn if it's one of the really bad, lobster-red, blisters-on-your-blisters kind. I wish I had sunnier news for you, but these are not the parental warnings you want to screw around with.

TRUE.

"I don't care if we're indoors, I hear thunder. Out of the pool!"

Water is one of the worst places to be when there's lightning nearby, unless you are hoping to recharge the flux capacitor in your time-traveling DeLorean and return to 1985. When you're swimming in open water, you're probably the highest point around, you're wet, and you're surrounded by an excellent conductor of electricity on all sides. That's just asking for trouble. Pools are somewhat safer, since swimmers are surrounded by points much taller than their own heads—the heads of all the unlucky nonswimmers! There have been cases of death or injury from swimming-pool lightning strikes, but most of the news accounts make clear that the victims were lounging *near* the pool or dipping their feet. Going inside is the best way to protect yourself from lightning, of course, but outdoor swimming pools don't seem to be the death traps you might imagine.

And yet, even many *indoor* pools insist on emptying the pool if there's the slightest rumble of thunder in the area. The YMCA's policy nationwide is to pull swimmers out of indoor pools until thirty minutes after the last thunder is heard, in accordance with the guidelines of the National Lightning Safety Institute. But even NLSI president Richard Kithil concedes that his organization "could find no reports of death or injuries in indoor pools related to lightning causes," and the Redwoods Group, the insurance provider that underwrites the Y, agrees on its website. Yet the evacuation orders persist.

This policy isn't just overly conservative, it might actually be harmful. Given the lack of indoor injuries on record, and the fact that I could find just one account of lightning striking an indoor pool *ever* (it passed through an open window and struck a Quebec pool in July 2000, causing no injuries), and the fact that electricity dissipates within about twenty feet of a lightning strike in water, it seems that a covered pool might be a comparatively safe place to be during a storm. Should lifeguards really be emptying these pools, knowing that many of the ex-swimmers will immediately head for more dangerous spots, like an outdoor parking lot? That would be like going out of the totally-cool-and-sitting-in-the-cupboard frying pan and into the fire.

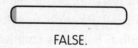

FALSE.

"Don't run around barefoot, you'll get worms!"

Abe Lincoln, Tom Sawyer, Opie—all the great American childhoods were spent barefoot. I spent as much of my elementary-school summer vacation sans footwear as possible—to this day, if I'm lounging around the house, the feeling of socks on my feet revolts me about as much as normal people would be revolted by the feeling of bugs on theirs. Seriously, when people tell me how much they love the cozy feeling of socks, I recoil like they've just told me about their collection of Third Reich tableware. Barefoot power!

But The Man (i.e., parents) doesn't want you playing barefoot during summer vacation, and often he'll trot out the specter of parasites. These little buggers, they tell you, will burrow into your feet and from there into your bloodstream and from there into your gut and then you poop them out endlessly to infect more people. Yuck. It's almost enough to send me out sock shopping.

If your parents gave you similar warnings, they were probably talking about hookworm, but here's the good news: unless you live in the developing world, hookworm hasn't been a problem in about a century. The CDC says that as many as three-quarters of a *billion* people worldwide have hookworm, but modern plumbing and sanitation have nearly eradicated the problem in North America. Eggs from the gut of a hookworm sufferer *can* hatch into larvae that burrow into bare feet, but that's only a problem in places where people are constantly pooping in fields or using human feces to fertilize crops. (Corollary: don't poop in fields or use human feces to fertilize crops.) "What about pet poop?" you might well ask. Dogs do get hookworm, but canine hookworm is a different species of beastie and has no interest in your digestive tract. In rare cases, hookworm larvae from dogs have infected humans, a condition called "burrowing eruption," but they just cause itching in the skin for a few weeks before dying out.

This doesn't mean that barefoot kids don't risk a lot of scrapes, blisters, and broken-glass encounters that could easily be prevented by a pair of Keds. But shoes come with their own health risks. Our feet evolved to be walked on au naturel, and there's plenty of evidence that sheathing them in leather and rubber hasn't been entirely positive. A 1991 overview by Lynn Staheli in the journal *Pediatrics* found that barefoot kids had stronger, healthier, more flexible feet than their shod compatriots, and a 2007 podiatry study found that two-thousand-year-old skeletons had better feet than modern shoe-wearers. We're devolving, people! For the fitness of the species, don't make your kids wear shoes during summer vacation until you've walked a mile without their moccasins.

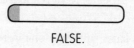

FALSE.

> ## "Was the nail you stepped on rusty? You'll get tetanus!"

The word "tetanus" comes from the Greek for "stretched tight," because infection leads to muscle contractions and spasms throughout the body—at first in the jaw, which is why it's also called "lockjaw." During the last century, it became an article of faith among doctors and parents that puncture wounds involving rusty nails were a particularly dangerous form of transmission. Among the famous tetanus victims killed by an encounter with one fateful nail were British ornithologist George Montagu, silent-movie cowboy superstar Fred Thomson, and Robert E. Lee's celebrated horse Traveller.

So I don't want to downplay the danger of nails: yes, puncture wounds can lead to tetanus, so kids should be vaccinated and adults should get their booster shot every ten years like they're supposed to. But the famous rusty nail is a red herring. Rust, of course, is just harmless iron oxide and doesn't cause infectious disease. Tetanus is spread by a hardy little bug called *Clostridium tetani*, which survives outside the body in the form of hardy little spores, much like anthrax. These spores are everywhere, so any kind of wound, from a deep scratch to an animal bite, can potentially transmit tetanus. There's nothing magical about the rusty nail, except that rusty nails are often dirty, and dirt can be full of tetanus spores. Hyping the rusty nail is dangerous: it may give parents a false sense of security when their little darling gets poked with something rust-free that may nonetheless be contaminated with tetanus.

The good news is that tetanus is now very rare (except in the developing world, where its neonatal form is still a serious problem). There are fewer than a hundred U.S. cases every year, mostly involving people who let their shots lapse, and only one in ten turns fatal. I'd guess that the Rusty Nail cocktail (Drambuie and Scotch!) probably kills more people every year than actual rusty nails do.

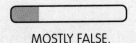

MOSTLY FALSE.

"Put On a Sweater, I'm Cold!" (Autumn and Winter)

> "Don't touch your Halloween candy until we get it checked out! There's always some sicko out there poisoning random trick-or-treaters."

The bogeymen of contemporary Halloween celebrations aren't ghosts and vampires and cackling witches, unfortunately. Instead, kids are spooked by a series of much more prosaic stories: "The Strychnine in the M&M's!" or "The Razor Blade in the Candy Apple!" or "The Pedophile Who Groped the Trick-or-Treater!" My childhood Halloweens came right on the heels of the infamous Tylenol-tampering scare of 1982, when poisoned consumer products were on *everybody's* mind. As a result, I never got to eat a single piece of Halloween candy until Mom and Dad had gone over the whole bag, looking for needle marks and razor blades and other imagined Vietcong booby traps. (And, I realize now in hindsight, stealing all the Snickers.)

My parents weren't the only ones. Since this hysteria reached its height in the 1980s and 1990s, many hospitals, fire stations, and police stations have begun examining and X-raying candy for nervous parents. The National Confectioners Association (a.k.a. "Big Candy") began an annual hotline to field reports of tainted treats. It's become common knowledge that these threats exist—that they're widespread, even!

But in reality, here are some things that are more widespread than Halloween poisonings:

- Death by elephant stampede
- Octuplets
- Being hit by a meteorite

That's because there hasn't been *a single reported case* of a Mad Halloween Poisoner in history. Sure, newspapers have been whipping up Halloween hysteria since the late 1950s, but read one of these scare pieces with a more critical eye, and you'll get giggles, not chills. A typical AP attempt from 1982 breathlessly warns parents that some Mount Holly, New Jersey, residents recently reported a burning sensation after eating a Reese's peanut butter cup! Not to mention the discount store in Germantown, Tennessee, that called the cops when a syringe was found "near a Halloween candy display"! (Really, let's be honest. How many Tennessee dollar stores *don't* have a used needle lying around in one aisle or another?)

Fresno sociology professor Joel Best has made a career out of debunking Halloween hype. He made a list of seventy-two poisoning cases reported by the media since 1958 and methodically followed up on each one. Not one turned out to be the work of a mythical mad poisoner. Best did find two tragic deaths of children related to Halloween candy, but in each case, the responsible party had used the urban legend to camouflage a very different crime (in one case, a Texas father who killed his son for insurance money, and in the other, a Detroit family trying to cover up an accidental overdose from Uncle Henry's heroin stash). In other words, there have been two more *fake* candy deaths in Halloween history than real ones! In many, many more cases, a child became ill or died from some totally unrelated cause around Halloween, leading to panic, unnecessary product recalls, and even police confiscation of trick-or-treat bags.

Best also found about the same number of cases reporting pins and other sharp objects in candy. In virtually every case, these turned out to be hoaxes or pranks or both. (I call them "proaxes"!) The typical scenario was a child who'd been raised on these scare stories claiming to have found a sharp object in an apple or candy bar in order to spook family members.

The modern version of the Halloween Maniac myth, the neighborhood pedophile, is just as overhyped. In recent years, many counties have become so worried about trick-or-treaters that they've imposed an October 31 house arrest on sex offenders or forced them to spend the evening at a parole office. But in 2009, South Carolina psychology professor Elizabeth Letourneau published a paper called "How Safe Are Trick-or-Treaters? An Analysis of Child Sex Crime Rates on Halloween." Letourneau and three collaborators had studied over sixty-seven thousand sex crimes and found that, even before counties cracked down, Halloween had long been one of the safest nights of the year from sexual abuse, perhaps because so many children are involved in group and family activities. "These findings raise questions about the wisdom of diverting law-enforcement resources to attend to a problem that does not appear to exist," they wrote.

So this is what it's come to: a world where most of my kids' friends attend a local "trunk-or-treat" in a church parking lot instead of going door-to-door. (Trunk-or-treating, for those who don't know, is just like trick-or-treating, except with cars instead of houses, lame decorations instead of awesome ones, and no fun instead of fun.) And all because of a bunch of stuff that never actually happened. When I was a kid, we knew who the real Halloween menaces were: the dentist on the next block who gave out toothbrushes instead of candy, and anyone who gave out candy corn or (bleargh!) *circus peanuts*. We knew that nobody would ever actually poison circus peanuts. What would be the point? How could you make them worse than they already are?

FALSE.

"Close the damn door! Are you trying to heat the whole outdoors?"

As I learned the hard way, here are some things you should not say when you leave the front door wide open and your father bellows, "Were you born in a barn?"

- "So? Jesus was."
- "MOOOOOOO!"
- "No, but Grandpa says I was conceived in one. What does 'conceived' mean?"

I was always skeptical, as a child, that the prompt closing of doors would affect our heating bill in any way. What's one single doorway, one little rectangle, compared to the vast surface area of a two-story home? Of all the places that air could go while kids are greeting the dog or scraping snow off their boots, really, how much of it is going to choose to pass through that open doorway?

The answer is actually "quite a bit," due mostly to air pressure. If I might correct your aggrieved father on one small point, the problem generally isn't the warm air rushing out, it's the cold air rushing in. (Hot air rises, so the lower parts of a building, where the doors are, tend to have lower pressure in the winter than the upper ones.) I don't know of any research involving absentminded children and single-family homes, but a 2010 Cambridge University study looked at shops that keep their front doors open during the winter months. Even though many retailers claim that their invisible "air curtain" keeps the warm air from escaping, the Cambridge engineers found that these devices actually use more energy than they save, and that a single shop's open door, during an average week of winter, has the same carbon footprint as a four-hundred-mile plane flight. The average store could cut its energy bill in half just by closing its front door.

In 2006, MIT grad students found that more careful door use could save seventy-five thousand kilowatt-hours of electricity in just one campus building. Revolving doors retain warm air eight times more efficiently than swinging doors do, so the study found that the building could lower its heating bills by 1.5 percent if everyone used the revolving door. Maybe MIT should hire your dad to stand by the front of the building and hector the revolving-door skeptics as they go in and out.

Obviously, the door in a private residence gets opened less than one in a public building, so I'm not sure how much higher your utility bills get every month once your children hit the born-in-a-barn phase. But even if the effect is small, parents are right on this one: leaving the front door open on a cold day does waste heat and create drafts. Oh, and *Home Energy* magazine says that 7 percent of your refrigerator's electricity use is due to grazers holding the door open while they idly wait for new snack options to materialize. Your parents were right about closing that door too.

TRUE.

"Bundle up or you'll catch a cold!"

With the common cold being so common and all—most people catch two to five every year, or up to ten if they're in the germ factory that is an elementary school classroom—you'd think we'd understand it a little better. For centuries, mothers have been saying that going outside with wet feet or without a scarf would lead to our "catching our death" of a conspicuously nonfatal illness. But the effects of cold-temperature exposure on colds are still poorly understood even by experts. It's a controversial morass of data as sticky and discouraging as the gunky, infected nose of a toddler in November.

First of all: some ground rules. Of course cold weather doesn't *cause* a cold. The actual cause of most colds, we've known since 1956, is the human rhinovirus. Variety being the spice of life, this family of germs comprises over a hundred different serotypes, enough to keep you coming down with new colds for a lifetime without ever developing a lasting immunity. Before disease transmission and treatment were well understood, people noticed that respiratory tract infections were worse in the winter and blamed the weather, which is how colds got their name. To this day, 38 percent of respondents to one survey blamed cold weather—not germs!—for the common cold.

It is undisputed that there is a "cold season" during the cooler months of the year, though we know now that rhinovirus colds are actually more common during fall and spring, while winter "colds" are more often a mild brush with a similar bug, like the flu. But there are several schools of thought on just *why* cold and colds go hand in hand. Some argue for environmental factors: during the colder months, people stay inside more and kids are back in school, increasing the odds of disease transmission. Others point out that the rhinovirus itself thrives at humidity levels that are more common during the winter. But more recent research is starting to center on the possibility that your grandparents were right after all and that exposure to cold makes *you* more susceptible to colds.

The most recent review of the relevant research was published by Eleni Mourtzoukou and Matthew Falagas of the Alfa Institute of Biomedical Sciences in Athens. They point to experimental evidence like that from Ronald Eccles at Cardiff University, who found that subjects given a chill by dipping their feet in cold water for twenty minutes were more than twice as likely to catch cold within the week compared to the control group. Several mechanisms have been proposed to explain the body's potential vulnerability to colds when things get chilly, but there's evidence in hypothermia cases that cold can both decrease and slow down the infection-fighting white blood cells circulating throughout your body. Cold can also cause vasoconstriction (narrowing of blood vessels) in your nose, where rhinovirus hangs out. This makes the hair-shaped cilia in your respiratory tract less effective at filtering out bugs.

But these findings aren't uncontroversial. Repeated clinical trials since the 1950s have shown that when you dab infected mucus (eww!) on someone's nose, the temperature at which you dab has no effect on whether or not they get cold symptoms. As a result, many doctors believe they've closed the book on the cold-weather-causes-colds quackery. But critics like Dr. Eccles argue that those studies were too artificial to model real-world cold transmission and that more studies are needed where colds are contracted, *outside* of a laboratory. I look forward to seeing more of this kind of research, and so should you, unless you are an infected-mucus supplier by trade.

Since so much about cold transmission is unknown, I'm going to come down narrowly in favor of bundling up. It certainly can't hurt—as long as you remember that not getting a cold in the first place is a smarter strategy than bulking up your immune response. Especially during cold and flu season, wash your hands frequently and avoid touching your face. When it comes to cold prevention, putting on mittens and a scarf are statistically insignificant compared to good hygiene. But hey, even a small edge on a nasty cold is nothing to sneeze at.

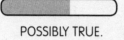

POSSIBLY TRUE.

"Put on a hat—most of your body heat escapes through your head!"

This old saw wasn't just made up by somebody's superstitious grandma—it actually has an authoritative-sounding source. A 1970 U.S. Army field manual for cold-weather survival claimed that 40 to 50 percent (not "most") of one's body heat is lost through the head in frigid conditions. It stands to reason, then, that a hat is indispensable if you're going outside, right?

Well, not so fast. The army's findings come from experiments it performed in the 1950s by sending soldiers out into subzero temps wearing arctic survival suits . . . . and no hats. Under those conditions, shockingly, lots of body heat was lost through the head! But, as a University of Louisville hypothermia expert named Daniel Sessler explained to *The New York Times* in 2004, you'd get the same results by leaving *any* body part uncovered. Our faces and necks are five times as sensitive to temperature changes as the rest of our bodies, so our heads may *feel* particularly vulnerable to cold on a winter's day, but you'd lose just as much heat by putting on a hat but leaving, say, an arm or a leg uncovered. Dr. Sessler estimates that if the army were to retry their field test with their subjects wearing only swimsuits, only 10 percent of body heat would be lost through the head, and a 2006 University of Manitoba study found similar results.

If your head is cold, sure, put on a hat, but it's not a magical cure-all. If your hands are cold, wear gloves; if your feet are cold, try socks or slippers. If your heart is cold, I recommend Internet videos of kittens.

FALSE.

"Don't eat snow—it'll make you sick!"

Frank Zappa warned us about the yellow snow, but his oeuvre is silent on the other possible colors of winter precipitation, including white, which I understand is the most common variety. Findings published by Louisiana State researchers in *Science* magazine in 2008 revealed that some snowflakes form around a "seed" of airborne bacteria like *Pseudomonas syringae*. At the time, this led to lots of scary headlines and "Why snow might be killing *your* kid!" teasers before commercials in local newscasts.

This was silly. *Pseudomonas syringae* does cause a fatal disease—in bean and tomato plants, not humans. Even if some snowflakes do condense around icy bacteria, the human stomach is acidic enough to take care of them. We live surrounded by microbes, after all, and they're found in *everything* we eat, not just snow. There's no need to go all Howard Hughes after every winter snowfall, since there's not a single clinical report in the medical literature of a kid getting sick from snow eating.

That doesn't mean that every winter snowbank is already 100 percent pure as the driven—er, it seems like there should be some weather-related analogy here. In any case, ever since the Industrial Revolution, there have been worse things in the air than plant diseases, and snow might contain any of them. Dr. Jeff Gaffney of Argonne National Laboratory ran down the list for the *Chicago Tribune*: sulfates, nitrates, sulfur dioxide, and even lead from parts of the world that still burn leaded gasoline. (It takes less than a week for industrial pollutants in the atmosphere to spread halfway across the globe.) You won't get dangerous amounts of any of this stuff by catching flakes on your tongue or licking snow off your gloves, but any kid tucking away repeated eight-course meals of snow might want to ease up.

MOSTLY FALSE.

"Stay away from the Christmas poinsettia! The leaves are poisonous."

The red blooms of the *Euphorbia pulcherrima* shrub were already a popular Christmas symbol in Latin America when they were introduced to the United States in 1825 by Joel Roberts Poinsett, the first American minister to Mexico. In Mexico and Central America, the flowers are still called "*nochebuena*," the Spanish name for Christmas Eve, and they decorate millions of homes and offices every holiday season on this side of the border as well.

This means that, every Christmas, millions of children are warned not to touch or taste the plant's red leaves, which two-thirds of Americans still believe to be poisonous. The truth is that you're probably safer eating an entire potted poinsettia than you are eating Grandma's holiday fruitcake. Unlike other plants in its genus, the poinsettia isn't dangerously toxic at all—not to people, not to pets. Poison control centers say that you'd have to eat about six hundred poinsettia leaves to get a meaningful dose, and even then the symptoms are no worse than an upset stomach. (Probably not much different from the upset stomach you'd get by eating six hundred leaves of *anything*.) Researchers at Ohio State put poinsettia plants in a blender and fed lab rats megadoses of the stuff in a 1971 experiment, and it didn't even affect the rats' appetite.

The myth of the poisonous poinsettia dates back to 1944, when a Honolulu physician erroneously reported that chewing on a poinsettia had killed the two-year-old son of a soldier stationed at Hawaii's Fort Shafter shortly after the First World War. But I still wouldn't recommend sprinkling the plant's leaves on your favorite holiday salad or figgy pudding. I tried a few last Christmas and they're terribly bitter.

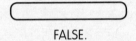

FALSE.

"Don't Make Me Get the **Other** Thermometer!"
(Sickness unto Barf)

"Feed a cold, starve a fever!"

This old wives' tale was probably already old in 1574, when a Welsh religious thinker named Lewis Evans added a list of proverbs to a popular English-Latin children's dictionary. Among his additions was the earliest expression of this dubious medical practice: "Fasting is a great remedie of feuer." Even though we've had over four hundred years to work on the phrasing of this myth, it's apparently still not catchy enough, since it's often quoted by people who can't quite remember which one—cold or fever—is supposed to be starved.

The answer, doctors agree, is neither. In the sixteenth century, colds were believed to be caused by chills, while fevers were associated with heat, so it made sense to fuel your inner fires with a big meal when you had a cold but not a fever. Now that we know how diseases are actually transmitted, we know that the immune system needs nutrition and fluids to fight all bugs, regardless of the symptoms. Your appetite may be suppressed sometimes when you're sick, but it's okay—that's the body's way of focusing its energies on immune response, not digestion.

In 2002, a team of researchers in Amsterdam made headlines with some findings that appeared to support the old folk wisdom. After a festive Christmas dinner, the scientists decided to take their own blood samples (wow, that's some Yuletide cheer!) to see what their drinking had done to their immune systems. The results showed that the food they'd been eating had a bigger effect on immune response than the alcohol, so they tried further tests, comparing the blood of six subjects after a big meal to their blood after a fast. They found that the well-fed patients had high levels of gamma interferon in their bloodstream, a sign of the body's immune response against viral infection, while the fasting patients showed higher levels of interleukin-4, characteristic of a different kind of immune response, the one the body uses for bacterial infection. Could this be the origin of "feed a cold, starve a fever"?

Doctors are unconvinced. Even for a study concocted by tipsy Dutch scientists after a rowdy holiday dinner, this one is a little suspect, since it was only performed on six subjects and has never been replicated. And some of the most common causes of fever, like the flu, are viral diseases as well, so the Dutch findings may not apply. If you're sick and you feel hungry, eat. If you're not hungry, don't eat. That's a lot more intuitive and easier to remember than the "feed a cold" thing.

MOSTLY FALSE.

"I'll bring you some chicken soup, you'll feel better!"

Penicillin wasn't discovered until 1928, when Alexander Fleming first used it to kill staphylococcus bacteria. But "Jewish penicillin," a.k.a. chicken soup, has been fighting disease a lot longer than that. The fourth-century B.C. medical text *De internis affectionibus,* sometimes credited to Hippocrates, recommends boiled chicken "in the case of purulent catarrh also from rotten cold." A few centuries later, Dioscorides, army surgeon for the Roman emperor Nero, prescribed "the broth of a chicken dressed simply . . . for restraining foul fluids, and for those who have hot burning stomachs."

You might assume that chicken soup's medicinal properties are mostly psychological: it's comfortingly warm, easy to digest, reminiscent of Mom and home, and salty enough to taste even through the worst nasal congestion winter can throw at you. But there have actually been small-scale studies of chicken soup's efficacy at treating colds, and the research is promising. In 1978, researchers at Miami's Mount Sinai Medical Center studied the noses of fifteen soup-eaters and found that airflow was unaffected, but sips of hot chicken soup increased "nasal mucus velocity" to 9.2 millimeters per minute, making it more effective at flushing out the nose than either hot water or cold water alone. The authors guessed that this might be due to chicken soup's "aroma . . . or through a mechanism related to taste."

An even more surprising result came from the Nebraska Medical Center in 2000, where Dr. Stephen Rennard studied blood samples from volunteers dosed with various chicken soups, including a homemade matzo-ball soup whipped up by Mrs. Rennard from a recipe handed down from her Lithuanian grandmother. In all cases, the soup inhibited the migration of neutrophils, the white blood cells that gang up on bacteria. (That's actually a good thing, since easing symptoms is most of the battle when it comes to cold relief.) Dr. Rennard hasn't followed up with clinical trials, but his results suggest that chicken soup may be an anti-inflammatory that soothes sore throat and congestion.

The soup you turn to for cold relief doesn't even have to be fancy, it turns out. The homemade Old World soup did just fine in the tests—better than a vegetarian control soup and much better than plain Nebraska tap water—but a few of the store-bought soups showed even better results. Don't tell Grandma.

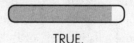

TRUE.

"You know what's good for that? Castor oil!"

This bit of parental advice might be more accurately termed "grandparental advice," since the generation that grew up on castor oil is past child-rearing age by now, I suppose. But castor oil is still the old-timey cure-all of choice in a multitude of old sitcoms, children's books, *Little Rascals* shorts, and *Tom and Jerry* cartoons. These references may leave modern audiences befuddled. How do you get oil from a "castor," and what is it supposed to do exactly?

Castor oil is an almost colorless liquid extracted from the seeds of *Ricinus communis,* a tropical plant. Some parents administered a spoonful of the oil as a weekly supplement, for its alleged-but-vague health-promoting properties. Others used it as an occasional remedy for any and all symptoms: colds, fevers, nausea, constipation. In many homes, it was the pharmaceutical equivalent of Lifebuoy soap: a harmless but foul-tasting punishment for bad behavior.

The fact that castor oil was used both as medicine and punishment should already be a red flag, but the truth gets worse. Today, castor oil's only FDA-approved internal use is as a laxative, but it probably shouldn't be your laxative of choice. It works by causing cramping of the bowels, which can have unpredictable and long-lasting results. (Not specific enough for you? All right, here goes: fecal incontinence, explosive diarrhea, powerful and uncontrollable bowel movements during sleep hours. Maybe I should have stuck with euphemisms.) In Italy, *usare l'olio di ricino* ("using castor oil") is still slang for coercion or abuse, because Mussolini's Blackshirts used to dose victims with the bowel-emptying stuff to humiliate and dehydrate them. Even worse, the castor bean is also the source of ricin, a poison so deadly that just a few salt-sized grains of it can kill an adult. Ricin was the poison used in the famous 1978 "umbrella murder" of Bulgarian defector Georgi Markov. The process by which castor oil is extracted supposedly keeps out the toxins, but I'd still think twice before dosing up a kid with it just because he can't poop.

The British may drive on the wrong side of the road and eat kidneys for breakfast, but their choice of disgusting children's oils has certainly aged better than ours. Since Victorian times, British children were lined up for a regular spoonful of good health in the form of cod-liver oil, a gooey liquid literally squeezed from the livers of fermenting codfish. It tasted even worse than castor oil, but unlike castor oil, it actually did some good: it was rich enough in vitamins A and D to ward off childhood diseases like rickets, and its high levels of omega-3 fatty acids have proven, in more recent studies, to help out with everything from ear infections to ADHD to arthritis. Their cure-all *actually* cures everything; ours is extracted from a neurotoxin and causes explosive diarrhea. Game, set, and match to the British.

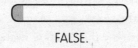

FALSE.

"Don't hold in a sneeze, you'll hurt your ears!"

Which is more annoying to your fellow human beings: the dainty, high-pitched, anticlimactic squeak of the sneeze-stifler, or the heartily bellowed "Achoo!" of the sneezer-with-gusto? That is a question of taste not easily answered by science. But you'd think science would have more to say on the health consequences of both styles. Despite the preponderance of parents and teachers warning kids about the dangers of suppressing sneezes, there has been surprisingly little research into the phenomenon.

The safest form of sneeze stifling, just as with contraception, appears to be abstinence. Not sneezing by preventing a sneeze—blowing your nose, pinching your upper lip, or whatever Jedi mind trick you prefer—is 100 percent safe, with no side effects other than watery eyes and possibly the need to sneeze again in a minute. (The abstinence metaphor holds!) But when it comes to suppressing a sneeze already in progress, whether by pinching your nostrils or sneezing into a closed throat, doctors tend to be skeptical. A sneeze projects particles out of your nose and mouth at over a hundred miles per hour. What happens if you decide to absorb all that pressure back into your head tissues instead?

There are cases in the medical literature of sneezing causing physical injury, including hernias, brain aneurysms, and nerve damage.

In 2004, star Cubs outfielder Sammy Sosa made headlines when he missed a game against the Padres due to back spasms caused by two pregame sneezes. But all of these cases that I could find were associated with violent, *un*suppressed sneezing. Alan Wild, a head surgeon and professor of otolaryngology at Saint Louis University, told the "Life's Little Mysteries" bloggers that a suppressed sneeze could conceivably injure the diaphragm, the eardrums, or the blood vessels in the eye and brain, but that all these outcomes were exceedingly unlikely. "The injuries that might occur are flukes or are related to some underlying anatomical oddity," he said. Unless you've had some kind of preexisting injury or surgery to your head or throat, there's no evidence that a stifled sneeze is any more dangerous than its louder counterpart.

Many medical guides advise patients not to hold in sneezes on the grounds that the stuff you're trying to eject could cause infections when propelled back into the sinuses and ears. This actually sounds more plausible than, say, a bruised eyeball, but it's never been studied in any kind of authoritative way. I am a lifelong sneeze-stifler who's never had an ear infection, but that's a sample size of one. Sneeze squelching may spread fewer germs and even pop fewer blood vessels, but more study is obviously needed before I begin teaching "Practice Safe Sneezing" workshops to middle-schoolers.

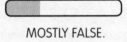

MOSTLY FALSE.

"You're better off catching chicken pox now—go play with your sick cousin!"

For centuries, the same parents who nervously bundled up their kids to protect them from colds would intentionally infect them with illnesses much more dangerous. If one neighborhood kid came down with the chicken pox (or mumps, or measles), children from miles around would be trooped into the sickroom in hopes that they'd get sick as well. Before vaccinations, this practice was at least defensible, because many of these diseases are more severe in adults than in children. If you're too old when you come down with them, the mumps can make you sterile, the measles can give you encephalitis, and chicken pox can lead to hepatitis or pneumonia. All were—and in rare cases still are—sometimes fatal for grown-ups, so it might have made sense to give your kids immunity as soon as possible. (But remember that these forced exposures no doubt led to the occasional tragic death as well.) If nothing else, it was a chance for parents to get all their kids sick at the same time, on a schedule of their choosing. The only thing worse than childhood disease is *inefficient* childhood disease!

Surprisingly, this kind of parental germ warfare still goes on in the twenty-first century, even though an effective chicken pox vaccine has been available for over fifteen years. "Pox parties" are popular with antivaccination types, who proudly infect their children with a week of flu symptoms and an itchy, painful rash in the name of "natural immunity." But this is getting harder now that the chicken pox vaccine is making cases of the disease rarer, so pox parties have entered the Internet age. In 2011, news reports broke of a national ring of parents using a Facebook group to swap and sell lollipops that had been licked by contagious chicken pox sufferers. Authorities took a dim view of this Jenny McCarthy–style bioterrorism, pointing out that sending viruses through the mail is a serious felony and that buying contaminated bodily fluids from a total stranger is a bad idea in general. Who knew?

Even by the science-challenged standards of the antivaccine movement, the chicken pox vaccine has turned out to be an enormous success. In the early 1990s, over one hundred Americans—mostly people with immunity problems—died every year from chicken pox. That number was down to fourteen deaths by 2007 and may continue to decline, as children are now given a second booster shot at age four that raises the vaccine's effectiveness to 98 percent. A mild rash in one in twenty-five children is the most common side effect, and not one death has been attributed to the vaccination in over forty million doses.

That hasn't stopped the "think outside the pox" crowd from objecting to the vaccine, on the grounds that it may not last as long as natural immunity does or might make adult outbreaks of shingles more common. (Shingles, a painful skin rash, is caused by a recurrence of the same virus that causes chicken pox.) But the vaccine has been given in Japan since 1988, so we already know it has more than twenty years' worth of effectiveness in it, and according to the Centers for Disease Control, the vaccine is actually proving to be *better* at preventing shingles than natural immunity. Good news, pox party animals: you can stop breathing on each other and then looking in the mirror for blisters. Science saved the day.

FALSE.

"Nope, nothing but soda! It'll settle your stomach."

When my siblings and I had the stomach flu, Mom was adamant: if we needed to rehydrate after puking out our guts, soda was the only thing we were allowed to sip. It's part of the universal Mom code. When you had an upset stomach, soda pop—the classic parental bogeyman of cavities, obesity, and eroded tooth enamel—somehow became a magical cure-all!

We call most kiddie stomach trouble "the flu," but it's not really influenza, the seasonal epidemic with a high mortality rate among the unvaccinated, the elderly, and *Downton Abbey* characters. Most cases of "stomach flu" in children are gastroenteritis, North America's second-most-common illness after the common cold. Staying hydrated is one of the trickiest and most important parts of dealing with gastroenteritis—thirty years ago, dehydration due to diarrhea killed over 4.5 million children in the developing world every year. But that number has been chopped down by two-thirds thanks to oral rehydration therapy, which administers water, sugar, and salts to patients suffering vomiting and diarrhea. When kids have upset tummies, they need the same stuff, but the Centers for Disease Control doesn't recommend soda pop as the way to go. "Substantial amounts of carbonated soft drinks . . . and other highly sugared liquids should be avoided," they advise, because too much sugar in your GI tract can cause osmosis, which will make diarrhea worse. A solution like Pedialyte is ideal, since it's not sugary and will replace the electrolytes you need. If a child is vomiting, start slow with just a few tablespoons, and slowly increase that dosage if it stays down. Fruit juice is okay too, but dilute it with water to lower the sugar load and avoid irritating the stomach. Oh, and you might want to choose a clear juice in case it comes back up. On a white sofa, for example.

A small amount of soda isn't going to kill you, but doctors say it has no special benefits and that the carbonation, far from settling the stomach, can actually cause bloating, the last thing you want when you're nauseated. Parents often swear by the stomach-calming powers of ginger ale, and it's true that many studies have proven ginger to be an antidote for motion sickness and the nausea caused by cancer treatments. But a can of supermarket ginger ale has only a fraction of the ginger needed for an effective dose. If ginger ale comforts you when you're sick, that's nice, but it's happening in your mind, not your gut.

The same killjoy CDC report that advises against soda also torpedoes the oft-recommended BRAT diet (bananas, rice, applesauce, and toast) for stomach trouble. This kind of thing is "unnecessarily restrictive and . . . can provide suboptimal nutrition," the CDC opines. Instead, children should be given their usual diet—or at least as much of it as doesn't end up spattered on the sides of a plastic wastebasket next to the couch where they are watching *SpongeBob*.

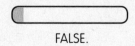

FALSE.

"Don't Pick at That!" (Bumps and Bruises)

"You need hydrogen peroxide on that!"

The medicine cabinet of yesterday was full of brown bottles with clinical-sounding names: iodine, hydrogen peroxide, Mercurochrome. They sounded painful, and when your parents applied them to a skinned knee, sure enough, they were. That's how you knew you were getting better! Feel the burn.

Well, you can't buy Mercurochrome anymore. It turns out the "Mercuro-" part means it's full of mercury! And it may *sound* like daubing toxic mercury on an open wound is a great idea, but doctors are now against it for some reason, so the FDA banned it in 1998. Hydrogen peroxide, iodine, and rubbing alcohol are still on store shelves, but the American Academy of Dermatology says not to put them on open wounds. (You've probably noticed that doctors still use iodine to disinfect skin—before a shot, say—but broken skin is another matter.) All three are irritating to healthy skin cells—that sting you feel is a sign that tissue is being damaged. Okay, I'll admit that hydrogen peroxide does look pretty cool when the enzymes in your blood make it foam like crazy, but what you're seeing is cells dying, capillary flow being restricted, and healing slowing down.

A widely circulated Internet list makes hydrogen peroxide out to be a miracle drug, good for everything from a stuffy nose to athlete's foot. In fact, the CDC advises against putting hydrogen peroxide on your skin and mucous membranes, ever. And it's not even a particularly good antiseptic! Hospitals use high-percentage hydrogen peroxide as a disinfectant but specifically warn against the household-grade stuff, which doesn't kill all the germs.

So if hydrogen peroxide is out, what's the best thing for cuts and scrapes? An antibiotic ointment like Neosporin on the bandage is fine, but doctors say the first thing to do is flush out the wound with a close cousin of hydrogen peroxide: dihydrogen monoxide, which is excellent at preventing infection and scarring. You probably know it as water.

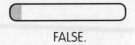

FALSE.

"I'll blow on the cut, it'll feel better!"

Actually it will. It will probably feel better. But science is continuing its long march to find fault with all of life's little pleasures, like bacon and asbestos. Blowing on a boo-boo is the latest victim.

"Do NOT breathe on an open wound," says the National Library of Medicine's health-advice website, complete with emphatic capital letters. It's common sense, I suppose: The mouth is full of bacteria. You're trying to keep an open wound free of bacteria. Putting the wound directly in the path of a bacteria stream might therefore be a bad idea.

That said, there's obviously no clinical literature detailing all the pus-filled infections that have resulted from Mommy blowing on an owie. Blowing on a wound is quite probably an extremely minor risk. In that case, given my tough stand on parental paranoia elsewhere in this book, why am I marking this one so vehemently false? Because in this case there are such easy work-arounds! Fan the cut with a piece of paper, run it under cold water, or use a cold compress, for crying out loud. Your germy germ breath isn't necessary.

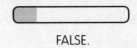

FALSE.

"Take off the Band-Aid and let the cut air out!"

(A warning if you are one of the many people who cringe at the word "moist": this entry is going to use the word "moist" a lot. Moist moist moist.)

Airing out a cut is classic Dr. Mom advice: how do you expect your wound to dry out and scab over if you keep it moist and gunky under a bandage? Take that Band-Aid off at least once a day and expose it to air.

Unfortunately, this advice has been outmoded since 1962, when a British doctor named George Winter published a groundbreaking study of moist wound healing in *Nature* magazine. Winter used a scalpel to make various cuts on the backs of young pigs and compared open-air to covered healing. Skin cells regrew about twice as fast on the moist wounds that weren't allowed to scab. Subsequent studies right up to the present have confirmed these results on human wounds. This means that you should keep a cut moist and covered for at least five days to regrow blood vessels and ease subepidermal inflammation. A drier environment will kill the very cells you're trying to grow back.

Antibiotic ointments are okay at first, but patients have reported side effects like swelling and itching with prolonged use, so you don't need anything fancy to heal well. A petroleum jelly like Vaseline is cheaper and will keep a cut nice and *moist*. Moist moist moist.

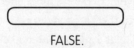

FALSE.

"Big kids don't cry!"

This well-intended admonition generally means "Try to get control of your emotions!" but it is, of course, not factual. Big boys and big girls cry all the time. A 2009 review of crying research by the German Society of Ophthalmology calculated that both men and women cry, on average, at least once a month: men cry between six and seventeen times per year, while women cry perhaps four times as often, thirty to sixty-four times per year. A more accurate but less catchy formulation for your kids might be something like "Big girls do cry, and are up to five times more likely to do so as a result of their menstrual cycle," or "Big boys do cry, especially during the last five minutes of *Saving Private Ryan* or *Field of Dreams.*"

The German review also found that boys and girls cry about the same amount until puberty hits, so old-fashioned moms and dads don't need to stress about a lachrymose little boy not having a "manly" control of his emotions. There are certainly times when children use tears as a tactic, and parents can use those moments to help kids identify their emotions and direct them in more appropriate ways. But most crying is harmless. They'll probably grow out of it, and most therapists say that adults benefit from an occasional cry anyway. A 2008 study at the University of South Florida found that 88.8 percent of respondents felt better after a good cry, and a 2011 study of NCAA football players found that the players who cried were more effective during games *and* happier off the field than the Eastwoodesque tough guys.

In 1972, a crying jag at a press conference famously submarined the presidential aspirations of Maine senator Edmund Muskie, but that stigma hasn't lasted in American public life. Nobody tsk-tsked when Michael Jordan cried after winning his first NBA finals, or *The Daily Show*'s Jon Stewart cried after 9/11, or Hillary Clinton cried on the 2008 campaign trail. (An alternate list for conservatives: Tim Tebow after losing the SEC championship, Jesus in John 11:35, Speaker of the House John Boehner every ten minutes.) It appears that culture and science have borne out the advice NFL great Rosey Grier sang to children of the 1970s on the album and after-school TV special *Free to Be . . . You and Me*: "It's all right to cry—it might make you feel better."

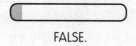

FALSE.

"It might be a concussion—we need to make sure you don't fall asleep!"

I got my bell rung on the playground once during second grade. I was running like a maniac and got slammed between two other kids who were also running like maniacs and down goes Frazier. Freeze Tag is the mosh pit of recess games. Someday it's going to get banned, like lawn darts.

Anyway, the teacher could see I was a little out of it when I got up blinking, and I had to sit with her for a few minutes in case I had a "concussion," a new word for me. She also wrote a note to my mom warning her to keep me from falling asleep. This was my first introduction to a scary bit of head-injury lore: you might hit your head and seem totally fine, but a little later you might drift into sweet, sweet sleep *and never wake up*! (Because you are dead.)

The idea that concussion victims shouldn't nod off is probably a result of the rare "lucid interval" that can accompany some head injuries. In these cases, the victim will be initially dazed, then appear to recover rapidly. But some unseen bleeding or swelling of the brain is going on unbeknownst to anyone, and a few minutes or hours later, their condition abruptly gets worse. Perhaps the most famous case of a lucid interval was the one that killed actress Natasha Richardson, Liam Neeson's wife. In 2009, she suffered what appeared to be a minor injury on the ski slopes; an ambulance was summoned but later sent away when she appeared to be fine. In a matter of hours, she was dead of an epidural hematoma.

But! These cases are very unusual, and doctors don't recommend sleep-depriving concussion victims because of them. If a head bonking is mild enough that no medical attention or hospitalization was necessary, then sleep is not the enemy. A 2005 study found that fatigue is a common side effect of head injury, which means that rest and sleep are probably what the body needs most to recover. Instead, we now have parents freaking out at postconcussion fatigue, because they believe it's the sign of some dire brain malady.

So let the kid sleep. You're the one who should stay awake. The National Institutes of Health recommends keeping an eye on concussion victims and, for the first twelve hours or so, waking them every two or three hours to make sure they know where they are and that their condition is unchanged. But that's just to make sure any unusual complication is caught in time, not because sleep itself is a dangerous complication. Actually, it might be the best medicine.

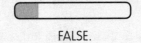

FALSE.

"If your nose is bleeding, don't lean your head back!"

Maybe your parents told you that you should always tilt your head back to stop a nosebleed. Mine were of the tilt-your-head-forward school, because leaning back *was dangerous*. Well, my parents must have been smarter than your hypothetical ones, because leaning forward is indeed the doctor-approved nosebleed position. Take *that,* your hypothetical parents! (If it's any consolation, I've seen my parents' yearbook photos and can almost guarantee that your parents were cooler in high school than mine.)

It's true that leaning your head back might stop your nosebleed . . . from coming out your nostrils. But it doesn't magically stanch or clot the blood flow. It just redirects it back down the throat or esophagus, which can lead to choking or nausea and vomiting. According to the American Academy of Family Physicians, leaning forward will prevent those outcomes. Sit down, tilt your head slightly forward, and keep your head above your heart. (Note to the American Academy of Family Physicians: This is the normal configuration of a sitting person. Do you treat a lot of circus acrobats?) Gently pinching the nose just below the bridge or applying a cold compress for five to ten minutes may stop the nosebleed, but most nosebleeds stop in five to ten minutes anyway, so this may be the first-aid equivalent of "If you treat a cold, it'll go away in fourteen days; if you don't, it'll last two weeks."

TRUE.

"When the scab itches, that means it's getting better!"

I've told my daughter this when an itchy scab is getting on her nerves, and now she informs us happily every time she has a cut or scrape that's starting to itch, because "it must be getting better!" She was also ecstatic last time I told her she was running a temperature, because apparently Mommy told her once that a fever means her body is fighting the sickness. I had to explain to her that this is true, but it doesn't mean a fever is a *good* thing. We warp our kids sometimes without even knowing it.

The fact is, I really had no idea if the itch of a healing wound was a healthy sign of healing or not, and it turns out doctors aren't really sure either. The mechanisms of pruritus, the scientific term for itching, are poorly understood—it can be as intense a sensation as pain, yet we understand pain much better. There's even disagreement over whether the same neural pathways that mediate pain are also the culprits behind itching. Itches come and go so capriciously that they're hard to study.

The itch of an injury can be caused by several things, some of which have nothing to do with healing. We know that the trauma of wounds and wound care can cause the body to release histamines, the same compounds that make mosquito bites itch. The drying of the skin may also be a factor. But another likely cause is the healing process itself: the closing of the wound, which can inflame nearby nerve fibers, and the irritation of a crusty scab pulling on a shrinking wound.

That doesn't mean only an itchy wound heals, though. Our parents may have sworn by the mystic curative power of the scab, but scabs lead to scarring (see page 43), so today doctors aren't fans. A small initial scab is fine to get the bleeding stopped, but after that, keep a wound moist, covered, and as scab-free as possible.

MOSTLY TRUE.

"Don't you dare pop that blister!"

My mom guarded the sanctity of her kids' blisters with the zeal of a pitchfork-wielding farmer defending his beautiful daughters' virginity. They were to remain intact *at all costs*! This of course runs counter to a child's first instinct: Hey, there's something new on my skin! What happens if I squeeze it?

But moms are right: blisters do heal better if you don't pop them. The fluid in a blister (actually serum, which is just blood with all the cells and clotting factor removed) and that thin bubble of skin are there to help damaged tissue heal. Open that up to the air, and you're asking for infection. The Mayo Clinic's first-aid guide recommends covering blisters with bandages and waiting for them to heal on their own. The fluid will just get absorbed back into the body once the burn or friction wound or whatever is better.

You should only pop a blister if there's literally no other choice, e.g., if it's too painful or impossible to walk on. Do this right and you can probably keep the bacteria out. Sterilize the blister and the needle with rubbing alcohol. (Many doctors no longer recommend sterilizing needles over flame, which kills bacteria but can leave carbon residue on the needle.) Prick the blister horizontally in a few places near its edge, leaving the overlying skin intact. Bandage and repeat if the fluid comes back. Then get some better-fitting shoes.

MOSTLY TRUE.

"Those are just growing pains!"

Wow, way to give your kids a complex, Mom and Dad. Growing up doesn't actually hurt. Well, it might hurt when your dad remarries and moves to a different state, or your best friend since kindergarten doesn't invite you to a middle-school sleepover, or when you drop your cafeteria tray and that girl with the long blond hair who smells like Hostess Fruit Pies totally laughs at you. Uh, just for example. But the *physiological process of growing* doesn't hurt at all.

That's right: scientists still have no idea what causes growing pains, but they're sure it has nothing to do with growing. We know this thanks to studies showing that these pains (a) don't correspond to actual growth spurts, and (b) are limited to muscle tissue, not to the bones or joints where growth actually occurs. The condition is so vaguely understood that nobody's even sure how common it is—researchers have found the incidence to range from 2.6 percent all the way up to 49.4 percent, depending on how they define and diagnose it. Various studies have suggested that growing pains might be related to poor posture, restless leg syndrome, bone fatigue, or even psychological issues.

There's no cure for growing pains, though one study found that an eighteen-month muscle-strengthening program helped ease them in many kids. While you're waiting for your kids' leg muscles to get toned, a rubdown or heating pad can also help reduce growing pains. Actually, about that name—the authors of a 2006 study from the University of Auckland in New Zealand suggested that, for accuracy's sake, we rename growing pains "recurrent limb pain in childhood." I like it, but apparently it's failed to catch on. Maybe Alan Thicke and Kirk Cameron are opposed to it. I sure wouldn't watch a sitcom called *Recurrent Limb Pain in Childhood*.

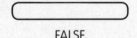

FALSE.

"Look Both Ways Before You Cross the Street!"
(Grievous Bodily Harm)

"Never run with scissors!"

Scissors have been mass-produced household items since the mid–eighteenth century, and I've seen dire parental warnings about running with them dating back to the 1880s. All parents, it seems, know a friend of a friend whose kid gouged out an eye or impaled a toe or something by not transporting scissors at a sufficiently leisurely speed. The expression "running with scissors" has, against all odds, become shorthand for rebelliously reckless behavior, like "living on the edge" or "playing with fire," and has been immortalized in several bestselling titles, including an Augusten Burroughs memoir and a Weird Al record.

Do injuries actually result when kids run with scissors? They do! The U.S. Consumer Product Safety Commission maintains a fascinating database called the National Electronic Injury Surveillance System (or NEISS), a statistical sampling of emergency room visits nationwide. NEISS estimates that 4,556 kids under ten sought medical care in 2010 for scissors-related injuries, none of which were fatal. About a hundred of those are the eye injuries that Mom and Dad always harped on. Some of the cases in the NEISS database include physician notes, and I found nineteen scissors-related cases since 1997 in which "running" was implicated. Those kids' moms and dads must feel like the worst parents in the world!

So I can't really tell you that scissors are completely safe. They are hard and metal and at least somewhat pointy, and if you fall on such an item, ouch. More to the point, it's hard to imagine a case where cutting something with scissors is so urgent that you'd have to run to do it. No one is ever like, "I need those paper dolls finished *stat!*"

But it's easy to demonstrate with NEISS that scissors aren't *especially* dangerous, certainly not in keeping with their gangsta reputation. Seventy-two percent of those 4,556 injuries were to fingers, it turns out, which means that *cutting* with scissors is a vastly bigger problem than running with them. Looking at scissors injuries to older kids since 1997, I was able to find doctors' notes on six patients who suffered "buttock lacerations" when they accidentally sat on a pair of scissors, compared to only four who were hurt running. But is "sitting on scissors" a slang term for wild, devil-may-care behavior? It is not!

If you've ever used the safety scissors that kids are around most often, you know that they have a hard time getting through construction paper, much less human flesh. It might be a good idea to remind kids that they should be more careful around Mom's sewing scissors than they are with those flimsy, rounded things that get passed out at day care. But overall, NEISS reveals that kids are downright safe around scissors compared to death traps like batteries (4,972 injuries last year), handrails and banisters (9,434), benches (11,563), and coins (28,674). Unless you shiver with fear at the sight of a banister, you don't need to teach kids excessive paranoia regarding scissors either. Why is a bench or handrail dangerous? Because you could trip and hurt yourself on it, just as you could with scissors or a pencil or a toy. It's the running around like a crazy person that leads to the accidents, not the scissors so much.

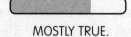

MOSTLY TRUE.

"Don't play with plastic bags—you'll suffocate!"

Some plastic bags *are* still dangerous to kids, but they're not especially dangerous to any kid old enough to heed a warning about them. Let's look at the numbers.

Parental awareness of the evils of plastic bags began in the late 1950s. The plastic shopping bag that's ubiquitous today didn't even exist then (it would be patented by a Swedish company called Celloplast in 1965), but plastic was just beginning to replace paper as the material of choice for large dry-cleaning bags. As a result, doctors and lawmakers began to note cases of children asphyxiating inside the bags and passed safety laws accordingly. The most detailed look at the danger was published in 1985 by UCLA epidemiologist Jess Kraus, who studied child suffocation deaths in California beginning in 1959, when the state passed a law mandating a safety warning on bags and prohibiting child-tempting cartoons on them. Over the next twenty years, he found, plastic bags were responsible for the deaths of 109 children in California, 23 percent of all child suffocations. The vast majority (79 deaths) were of infants less than a year old, and the remaining few were toddlers, with the exception of a couple of deaths of older kids using plastic bags to sniff glue. But Dr. Kraus found that the new safety laws and growing public awareness had worked: plastic bag deaths eventually dropped to one-third their former total, to less than one child in a million.

Today, the U.S. Consumer Product Safety Commission reports that plastic bags still kill about twenty-five American kids per year, almost 90 percent of whom are infants. The typical encounter involves a larger trash bag or dry-cleaning bag, which an infant crawls or falls into, or pulls over their face. That's obviously twenty-five deaths too many, but please note that garden-variety plastic shopping bags, the kind you're most likely to have around, are generally blameless, and older kids are safe around bags no matter what. If you don't have infants around, plastic bags are not a threat.

They are still an *ecological* threat, I should hasten to add. According to the Ocean Conservancy's National Marine Debris Monitoring Program, plastic bags make up a tenth of the junk washing up on our coastline. Because they're cheaper to produce than they are to recycle, up to a trillion of the damn things are made every year, which is probably a little excessive. If you switch to reusable cloth bags and skip, say, six plastic bags a week, that's 22,176 bags you're saving in a lifetime.

Not too shabby. My source on all this was a gentleman with a gray ponytail I just ran into at Whole Foods, but he seemed nice so I'll vouch for his statistics.

MOSTLY FALSE.

"Stand in the middle of the escalator or you might get sucked under!"

Why is the escalator warning sign longer than the instruction manual that came with my cell phone? So many rules for a twenty-second ride! Hold your kids' hands. Also, somehow, both handrails. Don't sit down. Don't wear flexible plastic shoes like Crocs, or an untied shoe, or God forbid, a scarf. Stay right in the middle of the escalator (while still holding your kids' hands, somehow). No carrying kids. No strollers. No playing. The signs make escalators sound like an Orwellian nightmare.

"Escalators are one of the safest forms of transportation in this country. The number of accidents is extremely small," explains Brian Black, an industry consultant who writes escalator safety codes. "But I use the analogy of a moving car. Cars are pretty safe, but that doesn't mean you want your kids crossing against the light."

How safe are escalators? The National Elevator Industry Inc., which is also the trade association for escalator installation and maintenance, estimates that Americans take 105 billion escalator trips per year. The NEISS emergency room numbers estimate 11,689 escalator-related injuries in 2010. That's almost doubled since 1997, but the reason is aging baby boomers, not kids. Over half of all escalator accidents nowadays are the elderly falling down. But even with the increase, a car trip is still sixty-three times more likely to lead to injury than an escalator trip. Escalators are very, very safe.

And they're getting safer. Escalators, according to Black, are now pretty foolproof even in the face of human rule-breaking. The skirts by the sidewall are more slippery now, so shoes don't get caught up against them, and brushes keep stray laces out. If something does get caught in the skirt or comb plate (that scary place at the top or bottom of the escalator where the stairs are absorbed into the floor), automatic switches with multiple redundancies will stop the escalator as soon as the blockage occurs. You won't get sucked under in gory fashion, like a movie villain getting devoured by sharks or army ants.

But don't get too cocky! Black also cautions that not all escalators will be up-to-date on safety codes or well maintained. (He cites the oft-malfunctioning escalators in public transit stations as the most common offenders.) So it's best to play it safe. Despite all the posted rules, when he watches families on escalators, he thinks parents are too blasé about escalator safety, not overcautious. Granted, this is a man whose professional expertise is imagining grisly escalator deaths, but still, it's not so hard to corral kids for the duration of a thirty-second escalator ride. I'm tempted to take his word for it.

MOSTLY TRUE.

"Don't talk to strangers!"

In 2005, a Cub Scout named Brennan Hawkins made headlines when he vanished on an overnight hike in Utah's Uinta Mountains. Four days later, miraculously, he was found by a search party—sunburned, scraped, bruised, and dehydrated, but thankfully alive. Parents and Scout leaders had taught Brennan the first rule of hiking safety: stay on the trail. And he did. How, then, did searchers manage to miss him for four full days?

Unfortunately, his parents had also drummed another rule into Brennan: don't talk to strangers. How could there be a better, less controversial rule of thumb for kids than this one, right? Who could possibly be against "Don't talk to strangers"? Well, the Hawkins family probably is, at least now. Brennan told his mom that, on many occasions, he'd seen groups of adults on horses and ATVs on the trail (no doubt looking for him). He took his parents' warnings to heart and ducked off the trail to hide when he saw "strangers"—every time. It almost killed him.

In her excellent book *Free-Range Kids,* newspaper columnist Lenore Skenazy debunks many of the myths of parental abduction paranoia and is surprised to find that the head of the National Center for Missing and Exploited Children (the same group that distributes the sad photos you see on milk cartons) emphatically agrees. "Our message is exactly the one you're trying to convey," he tells her. "We have been trying to debunk the myth of stranger danger."

Why are groups like the milk-carton people pushing back against "Don't talk to strangers"? "That message is not effective," says Molly Cirillo of the National Child Protection Training Center. In cases like Brennan's—or that of any kid who wanders off for five minutes at Target—children are safer when they feel comfortable seeking help from adults. And young kids have a hard time understanding what parents mean when they lecture about "strangers," because it's a tricky, abstract concept, defined only by who it *doesn't* refer to (people they know). Anti-helicopter-parenting advocates like Skenazy also worry about what kind of adults our increasingly stranger-insulated kids will turn into. What will they be able to do without their parents' constant protection? Will they be confident around new people? Will they be able to solve their own problems independently? "We need to help children develop their natural intuition about risk, and not give them overbroad rules," says security expert Bruce Schneier.

The most serious problem with "stranger danger" is that, statistically, it's completely backward. A Justice Department study from 1999 (the latest data available) found that eight hundred thousand Americans under eighteen are reported missing every year, which is where the scary "A child vanishes every forty seconds!" hype comes from. But the vast majority of these cases are runaways, and almost all the "kidnappings" turn out to be the work of a noncustodial parent or other relative or acquaintance. The stereotypical stranger kidnapper, the creepy trench-coat-wearer cruising playgrounds in his windowless van, does exist, but he only abducts one hundred and fifteen children a year. (That guy gets around.) There are over seventy million minors in the United States, so do the math. You wouldn't know it from media scaremongering, but any given minor is twenty-six times more likely to die in a car accident than to be abducted. And juvenile crime peaked in the early 1990s, so the kidnapping numbers are getting better, not worse.

By basing our fears and lectures around the mythical "stranger," we're freaking our kids (and ourselves) out about things that almost certainly will not happen, sometimes at the expense of more reasonable worries. So what is the right thing to tell kids about strangers? Molly Cirillo recommends leaving them out altogether. Teach kids that the real problem is "tricky people"—anyone, known or unknown to them, who tries to get them to break a safety rule (check with parents before going anywhere, take a friend along when you do, don't let anyone touch or hurt you). And if they get lost, make sure they know the best "strangers" to talk to: store employees, for example, or moms with kids in tow.

The only kind of "stranger danger" I'm willing to inflict on my children is a mortal fear of Billy Joel's 1977 album *The Stranger*. It's never too early to start teaching correct musical taste.

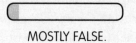

MOSTLY FALSE.

"Don't drop a coin from here—it'll fall so fast someone could get hurt!"

According to a long-standing urban myth, a harmless penny would become a lethal projectile if dropped off the Empire State Building, due to 102 stories' worth of gravity, the unstoppable, exponential compound interest of skyscraper accidents. If I may cut to the chase: yes, parents are right. It's a dumb idea to throw things off of high places.

But could a penny really kill you after a 1,200-foot fall? Not even close. In his book *How Everything Works,* physics professor Louis Bloomfield calculates that a penny's velocity at street level would be a whopping 210 miles per hour—in a world without air resistance. But air friction creates drag on falling objects, meaning they quickly reach terminal velocity, the speed at which air resistance and gravity balance out. A penny weighs only 2.5 grams and isn't shaped particularly sexily, so it would reach terminal velocity, about 50 miles per hour, after falling just a few stories. In practice, due to wind and updrafts, it would probably fall much slower than that.

When ABC News interviewed Bloomfield on the topic, they were unable to find a skyscraper that would let them test their math in person, so they improvised: Bloomfield attached a remote-controlled penny dispenser to a weather balloon and set it aloft. When the balloon was a few hundred feet in the air—well above the distance needed for penny terminal velocity—he began scattering pennies. They fluttered down slowly enough for him to catch, and he noted that when one caught him on the chin, "it was like getting hit by a bug." The *MythBusters* crew got the same result: even when they modified their penny launcher to fire at supersonic speeds, their human-skull target remained intact. At just about any speed, pennies are just too small and light to do the kind of damage that bullets do.

But Dr. Bloomfield warns that you shouldn't get cocky about air resistance: a slightly heavier or more aerodynamic object than a penny could do real damage. And even a penny can sting pretty good at fifty miles an hour—test this out by having someone throw pennies at you as hard as they can. If you're not a fan of the sensation, keep the change in your pockets next time you're looking down at a crowded sidewalk. You won't kill anyone, but you might make them say a swear.

MOSTLY TRUE.

"Watch out for those kiddie drugs that 'pushers' give out near schools!"

This is an urban legend that dates back to the "Blue Star acid" scares of the 1980s—and is still alive today, due to the magical powers of old people with e-mail! According to the scare lore, drug dealers back in the day sneakily disguised tabs of acid as transferrable tattoos decorated with blue stars and various cartoon characters, the better to hook kids on LSD. In his book *Curses! Broiled Again!,* urban-legend researcher Jan Harold Brunvand traces the hoax back to the 1960s circulation of "Snoopies," LSD-laced blotter paper that sometimes bore the images of cartoon characters. At least one state police bureau speculated that children might mistake them for tattoo transfers. Neither Brunvand nor anyone else has ever verified a single case of LSD tattoos actually existing, but that hasn't stopped hundreds of schools, day-care centers, and churches from distributing flyers on the menace. In the mid-1980s, the misinformation was so widespread that law-enforcement agencies started to worry that actual copycat incidents might spring up in response to the folklore.

The "Blue Star" rumors didn't really make a lick of sense, even if you assume some alternate-universe time warp where hippie drug pushers lurk outside school yards hoping to turn kids into "acid freaks." LSD isn't very addictive, it doesn't absorb through the skin very well, it's too expensive for fourth graders, and how would one accidental exposure via a tattoo win a drug dealer a new client anyway? How would the kid know that the tangerine trees and marmalade skies he was seeing were the awesome side effect of that picture of Popeye on his wrist?

But that hasn't made today's parents (and even cops!) any less gullible. In 2007, a similar media circus broke out over the specter of "flavored meth." Nevada officials had seized a brightly colored methamphetamine called "Strawberry Quick" and the Drug Enforcement Administration decided that children were at risk from the stuff due to its unusual fruity scent. "Drug traffickers are trying to lure in new customers, no matter what their age, by making the meth seem less dangerous," said a DEA spokesman. Other agents vouched for having seen chocolate and cola flavors. Meth disguised as Pop Rocks?! Parents went nuts. Headline writers went nuts. The Senate went nuts, unanimously passing the Saving Kids from Dangerous Drugs Act, which would double the penalties for making drugs seem delicious. Selling a pot brownie, in other words, would become twice as serious a crime as selling forms of marijuana less full of chocolatey goodness.

It turns out that candy-flavored meth was exactly as dangerous as "Blue Star" acid. In 2009, two years after the scare, a DEA laboratory *finally* uncovered a single sample of meth that appeared to have a grape lollipop crushed into it. The agency's bulletin, *Microgram*, reported that all the other colored meth samples turned in to labs by worried officers turned out to have no flavor or odor, and that the hubbub over kiddie meth had been "extensive and often alarmist." It now appears that a few scattered meth chefs were cooking up colored batches for branding purposes, and that escalated into a wave of "Won't someone *please* think of the children!" hysteria. In the case of the Saving Kids from Dangerous Drugs Act, that hysteria might still become federal law. Won't someone *please* think of the legislative integrity?

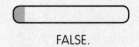

FALSE.

"If you crack your knuckles, you'll get arthritis!"

For many years, doctors would tell patients that their mothers had been right all along: don't pop your knuckles unless you want to develop arthritis in your hands later in life. In other words: to crack is wack. The clinical underpinning for the myth is easy to understand. Joints do tend to get creakier and noisier as they get old and arthritic, so some doctors reversed the cause and effect, just to be on the safe side: if arthritis can cause joint noise, why not the other way around? It's even easier to see why a parent would endorse this myth: knuckle popping can quickly get annoying, and moms and dads have long sought to squelch annoying little behaviors by linking them to medical threats. This is why I tell my kids that knock-knock jokes cause colon cancer.

Knuckles pop, most doctors believe, because the finger joints are surrounded by a lubricating liquid called synovial fluid. When the joint is extended, the pressure in there gets lower, and gases like carbon dioxide come out of solution and form a bubble. The big bubble quickly collapses with an audible "pop," but X-rays of recently cracked knuckles show tinier bubbles that stick around for another twenty minutes or so, before they're reabsorbed into the fluid. This is why you can't get a good crack out of the same knuckle twice in quick succession.

In recent decades, crack research teams have begun to study the arthritis connection in detail. In 1975, a UCLA professor polled nursing-home residents and found no connection between poppers and arthritics. (He took up the subject on behalf of his twelve-year-old son, tired of Grandma's constant warnings of rheumatism.) A 1990 study on a larger sample group came to the same conclusion—with the added caveat that knuckle popping did appear to correlate with slightly lower grip strength. The seniors who cracked didn't have any more joint pain than you'd expect, but they did need more help opening pickle jars.

The most thorough work in this area has come from Donald Unger, a California allergist who was, he said, pestered throughout his life by "his mother, several aunts, and, later, his mother-in-law" to *quit that damn cracking*! Instead of knuckling under to his critics, Unger tackled the problem firsthand: he spent the next fifty years cracking the knuckles on his left hand at least twice daily, but never those on his right hand. Thirty-six thousand cracks later, he finally published his study in *Arthritis & Rheumatism* magazine: he had developed no arthritis in either hand. For his half century of labor, Unger was awarded a 2009 "Ig Nobel Prize," an honor given at Harvard every year for dubious scientific achievement. "Mother, you were wrong!" he cried at the ceremony, gazing up into the heavens. Then he left the stage, clutching the award in his grossly swollen left hand. (Just kidding. His hands are identical.)

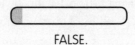

FALSE.

"Always wear a helmet when you ride a bike!"

Unless you travel in hard-core cycling circles, you probably don't even think of this as a point of controversy. It stands to reason that if you plan on hitting a curb with your head, or scraping your face along a few feet of asphalt, you'd rather do it with your skull encased in plastic and polystyrene foam. But in practice, that very simple observation tends to get overshadowed by other issues. Many cyclists find helmets uncomfortable, heavy, inconvenient, and restrictive of movement and vision. Others of a libertarian bent object to helmet use being mandated by law, whether it's a good idea on its own merits or not.

There's been endless study of the effectiveness of bike helmets since they started to catch on in the 1970s, and endless squabbling over the results. The best test would be a randomized controlled trial:

randomly assign thousands of cyclists to wear helmets or not, and track them all down later to compare injury numbers. But that's so impractical (and possibly unethical) that it's never been attempted. Case-control studies (comparing head injury victims to other hospitalized cyclists) always show strong benefits for helmet use, suggesting that it can reduce the risk of head injury by as much as 85 percent, but the anti-helmet crowd always pounces on methodological issues here, claiming (for example) that helmeted riders get injured less because safe, conservative cyclists tend to wear helmets, not because helmets are so awesome. Population-wide studies have shown more helmet-skeptical results. In 2006, Dorothy Robinson, a University of New England statistician, crunched numbers from New Zealand, Australia, and Canada before and after helmet laws were enacted and found that injury rates didn't decline, but bike use did. Robinson speculated that the protective effect of a helmet might be balanced out by other factors that lead to more accidents: helmeted cyclists feeling safe enough to try riskier stuff, for example, or the drop in the number of cyclists on the road, allowing drivers to be bigger jerks. (That last possibility was backed up by an interesting 2007 study in England that suggested that passing drivers gave three inches less clearance to cyclists wearing helmets.)

But when it comes to kids, these debates on the population-wide effects of bike helmet laws are red herrings. Parents aren't policymakers—they're only interested in the simple question of whether their kids' noggins are better off protected by foam when they bump into something, and those bumps will be *very* common. The Children's Safety Network reported in 2009 that children under fifteen made up 53 percent of the bike injuries in America's emergency rooms, and that young people were three times likelier than the rest of the population to suffer nonfatal cycling injuries. The effectiveness of helmets in high-speed vehicle collisions may be controversial in some circles, but even opponents agree that helmets are most effective in simple, low-speed falls—exactly what kids need. As a result, helmets are currently mandatory for kids in twenty-two states and hundreds of communities, and are strongly endorsed by the American Medical

Association and the National Safety Council. Even better, the helmets make their heads so gigantic and cute!

TRUE.

"Never play around refrigerators—you'll get trapped inside!"

Today, this advice can be revised to "Never play around refrigerators—they aren't very fun." But it's true that the first three decades' worth of fridges were genuinely dangerous. From 1927 to 1958, most refrigerator doors closed with a mechanical latch from the outside, which on occasion led to fatal games of hide-and-seek: kids would climb into an abandoned fridge and be unable to climb out. Refrigerators are airtight, of course, and too often the trapped children would suffocate before they could be found. In the summer of 1953 alone, thirty children died this way.

The refrigerator industry complained that removing latches and doors from old fridges was the consumer's job and that there *was* no foolproof device that would keep a refrigerator's cold-air seal but could still be opened by a push from the inside. But Congress got to work on a bill to outlaw latch doors and even considered siccing the National Bureau of Standards on the scientific problem. In the end, a design for magnetically sealing doors—a solution General Electric insisted wasn't ready for prime time—was pressed into service, President Eisenhower signed the Refrigerator Safety Act of 1956, and manufacturers fell in line by October 1958, when sales of the old death-trap fridges were officially banned.

There were still millions of the old fridges sitting in kitchens and basements, so reports of refrigerator asphyxiation continued to trickle in over the next few decades, but I'm still puzzled about the PSAs and full *Punky Brewster* episode about dangerous fridges that I was subjected to as a child in the mid-1980s, when the relevant menace had been illegal for almost thirty years. Today there are still occasional reports of refrigerator deaths in other countries with less stringent regulation (two kids in the Ukraine in 2007, another pair in South Africa in 2011) and a few similar incidents in the United States involving other airtight items not covered under the 1956 law, like linen chests and camper iceboxes. But the cold, hard fact is that U.S. refrigerators have been child safe for fifty-five years. Climb in and see for yourself.

FALSE.

"You're too young to lift weights. It'll stunt your growth!"

For many years, there was a widespread belief in the fitness community that kids shouldn't lift weights until they were fully grown, because strength training could damage their epiphyseal junctures— the "growth plates" where bones lengthen. The origin of this belief appears to be a report delivered by two Japanese researchers to the International Congress on Sports Sciences in 1964. The authors noted that children in remote Japanese villages were unusually small of stature and blamed this on the heavy loads they were made to carry as part of their daily chores.

That's quite a logical leap, and modern critics have pointed out many other reasons why poor children from mountainous rural areas made to perform backbreaking labor all day might not grow as tall as their city peers (hint: health care, diet). Many studies in more controlled environments since then have shown no such danger. In a 2001

Israeli study, for example, two groups of nine-year-olds were tracked for two full school years, with one group tackling a moderate-intensity resistance-training workout twice a week. The iron-pumpers, despite their young age, got considerably buffer, without sacrificing an inch of height.

It's true that before puberty, kids don't gain the same proportional muscle from lifting weights that a teen or adult would, but Dr. Avery Faigenbaum, a noted pediatric exercise specialist, points to studies in which children as young as six have benefited from strength training and says that, on average, kids show a 30 to 40 percent strength gain when they start lifting for the first time. Muscles aren't the only goal, of course; various studies have also shown that kids who weight-train have healthier bone density, body composition, cardiovascular fitness, and even resistance to injury. The risk of injury is, of course, one reason parents worry about kids and weights, but as long as the little bodybuilders are properly supervised to prevent overtraining and possible musculoskeletal injury, the American Academy of Pediatrics, the President's Council on Fitness, and *many* other groups say the rewards outweigh the risks.

Stunting kids' growth is *not* one of those risks, however. After all, David Robinson, Lou Ferrigno, and Shaquille O'Neal are all athletes who started lifting weights in their early teens. Do we really think those guys would be even taller if they'd stayed out of the weight room?

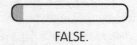

FALSE.

"You Don't Know Where That's Been!"
(Things Not to Put in Your Mouth)

"Don't eat your boogers, it's bad for you!"

Parents would be on firmer ground with "Don't eat your boogers, no one will want to sit by you in music class; bat after you in Little League; or hang out with, date, or marry you, and you will die alone with your cats." That is all 100 percent true. But is it really a health risk?

The societal taboo against eating boogers (or automucophagy, if you prefer to make it sound like a sex perversion) is much stronger than the taboo against mining them. A 1995 *Journal of Psychiatry* study of anonymous Wisconsinites found that 91 percent outed themselves as current nose pickers, but only 8 percent would cop to eating the results. In 2001, Chittaranjan Andrade and B. S. Srihari found a similar gap among Bangalore high schoolers and won an Ig Nobel Prize for their probing look into the nostrils of India. Andrade traveled all the way to Harvard to collect the award, joking, "Some people poke their nose into other people's business. I made it my business to poke my business into other people's noses."

Andrade and Srihari, mystified by earlier findings that "persons do eat nasal debris, and find it tasty, too," reported that "there isn't any significant nutritional content in nasal mucus." But Austrian lung specialist Friedrich Bischinger, quoted in 2004 wire reports, disagrees. He advocates nose picking to his patients, on the theory that the finger can "get to places you just can't reach with a handkerchief, keeping your nose far cleaner." And eating the evidence? Even better! "In terms of the immune system, the nose is a filter in which a great deal of bacteria are collected, and when this mixture arrives in the intestines it works just like a medicine," he says. "Modern medicine is constantly trying to do the same thing through far more complicated methods. People who pick their nose and eat it get a natural boost to their immune system for free."

Dr. Bischinger imagines a new utopia in which children are encouraged to pick their noses and society supports them in their nasal-excavating endeavors. But until we reach that distant shore, please continue to wipe your boogers on the undersides of desks and counters like God intended, instead of popping them in your mouth. At least when I'm looking.

FALSE.

"If you swallow watermelon seeds, they'll grow in your stomach!"

In 1993, this nightmarish scenario graduated from campfire lore to the august pages of the *Weekly World News,* so you probably won't be shocked to hear that it's botanically impossible. It's easy to see why watermelon is usually the fruit of choice in this myth: its slippery seeds are often swallowed intact accidentally, and the size of the resulting fruit makes the possibility of a gastric germination seem especially grisly. The fact that we rarely eat watermelon seeds in the West adds an air of exoticism to the idea of accidentally consuming one, but watermelon seeds, rich in protein, are actually a common food in many places. The Chinese roast and munch them like peanuts, while Nigerians make soup out of them. Dyed bright red, they're the traditional snack at a Vietnamese New Year party.

Until a sprouting seed grows its first leaves, it gets all its energy from aerobic respiration. There just isn't enough oxygen in the gastrointestinal tract for germination to occur, even if the stomach *weren't* also full of seed-killing hydrochloric acid. Dr. Gordon Rogers, a watermelon horticulture expert from Sydney, points out that this is all part of nature's grand design. "The whole purpose, really, of the watermelon fruit is for seed dispersal," he told a reporter investigating the myth in 2006. "They're designed to pass through the animal's gastrointestinal tract intact." In other words, a plant species will only thrive if its seeds sprout *after* an animal poops them out, not before.

Occasionally, you'll read news reports of a seed germinating inside someone's body, but these are always seeds that got accidentally aspirated into the trachea. (Unlike the digestive tract, the bronchi and lungs are oxygen-rich and acid-free.) My favorite case like this was a 2009 news report about Artyom Sidorki, from the Ural Russian city of Izhevsk. Mr. Sidorki was coughing up blood, and doctors ordered a biopsy, sure he had lung cancer. Instead of a tumor, they found a two-inch fir tree inside his left lung, evidently growing from an accidentally inhaled seed. "I'm so relieved it's not cancer," said Sidorki, obviously a glass-is-half-full type. I was able to find an 1890 report in the *Maryland Medical Journal* of a young child who accidentally aspirated a watermelon seed, which lodged in one of her bronchi. No full-grown fruit resulted, but doctors noted that "the seed had made an aborted attempt to grow." So make sure those watermelon seeds get all the way down, kids. Huff them into your lungs and there's no telling what might happen.

FALSE.

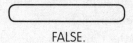

"Those silica gel packets in pill bottles are poisonous!"

What do a pair of shoes, a new cell phone, a bottle of Flintstone vitamins, and a bag of Korean shrimp crackers have in common? They're all likely to come with a little bonus tucked inside: a tiny white envelope marked with urgent-looking "DO NOT INGEST!" warnings in pink or pastel blue. What are these things? And if they're so perilous, what are they doing in my aspirin bottle?

Panic not. The little beads in these packets are made of a completely inert mineral, silicon dioxide. You know it better as sand or quartz. The beads are riddled with millions of micropores, allowing them to suck up 40 percent of their weight in water and thereby extend the shelf life of consumer goods. But if the contents of the envelopes are so safe, why do they always bear those mom-terrifying warnings? Because we're a litigious society. Munching on silica gel wouldn't do anything worse than make you a bit thirsty, but you could choke on the package, and manufacturers don't want to get sued for that. That's right: the little envelope is actually more harmful than the desiccant within. The same advice holds for pets: according to the ASPCA, the only danger is your pet getting the plastic packet stuck in its throat or digestive tract.

But the word isn't getting out: the Pet Poison Helpline notes that eating silica gel packets is the eighth-most-common report it gets from dog owners. And in 2009, over thirty-four thousand people called poison control centers because their kids had snacked on a packet. Poison control centers typically don't care, but they might ask if the gel was the blue "indicator" kind that turns pink when it gets wet. These beads are coated with a small amount of cobalt chloride, an additive that was linked to heart disease and possibly cancer when it was used as a beer-foam stabilizer back in the 1960s. But your kids would have to down the blue stuff like Pixy Stix to do more than upset their stomachs. And the blue beads are rare in American markets today, since the European Union banned them back in 1998.

Bottom line: if you're trying to injure yourself with a medicine bottle, the desiccant's not going to do you any good. OD on the pills instead.

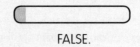

FALSE.

"Swallowed gum sits in your stomach undigested for seven years!"

Could this really be true? If I swallow a piece of gum today, will it really emerge, Rip Van Winkle–like, into some futuristic Japanese-style toilet in the year 2020? Is there a possibility that tonight I will poop the piece of gum I accidentally swallowed during *Big Momma's House 2*? When pondering these questions with my friend Raj, he remembered that as a child, he wondered what would happen if he swallowed *two* pieces of gum—would they be trapped for seven years or fourteen? In other words, would they serve their sentences consecutively or concurrently?

I hate to pop your bubble, but the answer is neither. Swallowed gum routinely gets furloughed within twenty-four hours, like a diplomat or a Kennedy. It's true that about a quarter of chewing gum is the gum base itself, a completely food-free substance made up of latexes, resins, waxes, and emulsifiers. Your gastrointestinal tract *could* work on that for years and have no luck digesting it. But that's not what happens.

"That would mean that every single person who ever swallowed gum within the last seven years would have evidence of the gum in the digestive tract," Dr. David Milov told *Scientific American*. "On occasion we'll see a piece of swallowed gum" in a colonoscopy, he said, "but usually it's not something that's any more than a week old." Your intestine eliminates gum the same way it eliminates half-chewed corn kernels and anything else that's too tough to digest: out the rectum within a day or two.

However, Dr. Milov also led the team that published the landmark study "Chewing Gum Bezoars of the Intestinal Tract" in a 1998 issue of the medical journal *Pediatrics*. A "bezoar" is a clump of undigested stuff that gets trapped in the stomach or intestine. (The wonderful name comes from a Persian word for "antidote," since animal bezoars, sort of like those owl pellets you had to dissect in eighth grade, were anciently thought to have remarkable health properties.) Most bezoars are boluses of food or pills; sometimes, in rare cases of "Rapunzel syndrome," they're made of swallowed hair. And sometimes, very rarely, they're made of chewing gum.

Dr. Milov's team found three cases of young children whose "means of discarding their gum (swallowing) was well known to the families and was a source of levity." Well, nobody was laughing when the gum swallowing led to chronic constipation and, finally, surgery when laxatives proved powerless. If you want your kids to quit swallowing their gum, here's the money quote:

> This clean-out regimen produced no results after 4 days. On the 5th day, the child was brought in for manual disimpaction under conscious sedation and rectal suction biopsy. On removal of the leading edge of the fecoma, a "taffy-like" trail of fecal material remained in the rectum. This mass was eventually manually withdrawn and was primarily made up of chewing gum.

Wow. I hope these parents kept the "rectal suction biopsy" video on hand to show future prom dates. But keep in mind: this was a kid who swallowed five to seven pieces of gum *per day*. Other cases only got serious when stuff like coins got swallowed and trapped in the Wrigley's-brand butt plug. So don't worry—the occasional accidentally swallowed piece of gum isn't going to do any harm. You'd have to be the Hunter S. Thompson of gum swallowing to get into medical trouble.

But prepare to be embarrassed if you're caught! Dr. Milov writes that "the rainbow of fused, multicolored gum fragments in the removed fecoma is easily recognized by physician and family as old gum." Maybe I'm just weird, but that actually sounds sort of beautiful—other than the part where it, you know, gets pulled out of someone's butt.

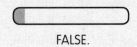

FALSE.

"Don't suck helium out of those balloons, it kills brain cells!"

I want to be very clear here. People who suck helium out of the balloons at birthday parties are at incredibly high risk—*of hilarity*! Because what could be funnier than people with normal voices suddenly sounding like Donald Duck and saying stuff? Nothing. There is nothing funnier.

But just try telling that to antidrug groups like the National Inhalant Prevention Coalition or the Partnership for a Drug-Free America, who routinely pitch a fit when "helium voice" is portrayed in the media. They successfully protested a popular 2000 FedEx ad in which some deep-voiced Munchkins get their squeaky mojo back using balloons, as well as a 2003 Toys "R" Us spot in which the chain's giraffe mascot takes a hit. Finally, in 2010, Geico stood up to this killjoy thuggery and refused to pull an ad in which an opera singer belts out a helium-enhanced aria.

The sternness of the scolding in these controversies might give you the reasonable impression that helium gas is actually dangerous in some way. But read more closely: the quotes are always cagier than that. "Younger children are at most risk of abusing inhalants," a spokesperson will say, carefully glossing over the difference between dangerous inhalants (furniture polish, paint thinner) and *completely inert* ones (helium).

That's right: helium gas, in and of itself, is harmless. As a kid, I always assumed the gas was changing your voice by doing something physically to your vocal cords, making them smaller or tighter or something. That's actually not the case. Your vocal cords are vibrating the same as always, but those vibrations are now traveling through a much lighter medium. As "Straight Dope" columnist Cecil Adams has explained the phenomenon, "You are effectively increasing the speed of the sound of your voice." The only nasty side effect of breathing helium is that it *isn't* oxygen. If you breathe nothing but helium for a minute or two, the lighter gas will displace the oxygen in your bloodstream, you'll get light-headed, and eventually you'll pass out. If you've read news stories about scary-sounding balloon-sucking incidents at birthday parties, that's probably what happened—somebody got dizzy and bumped his head on a coffee table.

U.S. Poison Control Centers reported two helium-related fatalities between 2000 and 2004, so it is possible (though apparently difficult) to find more dangerous things to do with the noble gas. The serious cases are usually ones in which idiots tried to suck helium out of a pressurized tank (which can lead to burst lungs and hemorrhage) or put their heads entirely inside a large helium balloon (which can lead to asphyxiation). But a little supervised helium sucking from a party balloon is perfectly harmless. There's no "high," so I don't think a helium balloon is a very likely gateway drug into glue sniffing. We don't keep kids with colds from using nasal sprays, following the same drug-paranoid logic. In fact, a helium-oxygen mixture (usually in proportions of about 80/20) has been used by doctors for decades to help patients who are having trouble breathing—the lighter gas is easier than air to inhale. Deep-sea divers sometimes use the same mixture. They may talk funny, but they breathe better, so it's worth it.

If helium, a lighter-than-air gas, makes your voice resonate faster, will a heavier gas make it slower? Yes! You can lower your voice by inhaling a gas like xenon or sulfur hexafluoride from a balloon (a party store will be no help here—you'll have to try an industrial-gas company). Sorry, guys: the rich masculine tones won't last long enough to get you through a job interview or first date. But your lungs are pretty efficient at mixing gases, so don't believe any alarmist hype about xenon gas pooling inside you. It's just as dangerous as helium—which is to say, not dangerous at all.

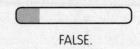

FALSE.

"Apple seeds are poisonous!"

When I was a kid, my friend Andy would amaze the cafeteria by polishing off an entire apple—stem, seeds, and all. To this day, I think that was pretty bad-ass and sometimes wonder if his trademark stunt is where the word "hard-core" comes from. (This is not where the word "hard-core" comes from.)

Andy may have been more of a daredevil than he knew, because apple cores do contain a potentially lethal poison—and not just any poison, but one of the sinister Agatha Christie ones! Apple seeds, like cherry pits, peach stones, and many other fruit seeds, contain a glycoside called amygdalin, which the body breaks down into sugar and hydrogen cyanide when ingested. Hydrogen cyanide prevents your cells from using oxygen, and even a tiny quantity can cause death within minutes. There is no antidote.

So how have we survived all this time with these ticking red time bombs in our midst, disguised as wholesome, keep-the-doctor-away snacks? Dosage! The body can metabolize minuscule amounts of cyanide over time, so a fatal dose would have to be delivered all at once. The average fatal dose of amygdalin in rats has been determined to be 880 milligrams per kilogram of body weight. (That ratio may differ for people, but it's harder to get funding to do the fatal-cyanide-dose test on humans.) A child weighing 75 pounds (34 kilograms) would need 29.9 grams of amygdalin to do the job. Apple pips weigh maybe 0.7 grams apiece and are about 2 to 3 percent amygdalin by weight. My math says an older kid would have to eat about 1,700 apple seeds to reach the rat-lethal dose. Oh, and the kid would have to chew them all really good to get through the tough kernel into the delicious, cyanide-rich fibers beneath. As we've discussed before, seeds are engineered to get through our systems intact when not chewed properly, and apple seeds are no exception.

It takes about six cups of well-chewed apple seeds to take out a kid, but I'm still inclined to call this factoid "mostly true," because it turns out that people are stupid. The supposed anticancer miracle drug Laetrile is a semisynthetic cousin of amygdalin made from apricot pits, and its toxicity got it banned by the Food and Drug Administration in 1980, but that hasn't stopped desperate people from gulping down thousands of dollars' worth. You can still find it easily for sale on the Internet, sometimes under goofy names like "Vitamin B-17." (It is not a vitamin.) I know cancer sucks, but it's important to remember two things about Laetrile:

1. It hasn't been effective against cancer in its only two clinical trials, according to the National Cancer Institute.
2. *It's a form of cyanide poisoning and has killed people!*

Apart from those two details, I guess it's all right.

MOSTLY TRUE.

"Thumb sucking is bad for you!"

This was an open question back in the 1950s, with psychologists at war against their natural enemies, the dentists. Dentists would claim that a thumb-sucking child was doing serious damage to his palate and teeth. Psychologists would counter that *preventing* a child from sucking his thumb did even more serious damage—to the child's fragile psyche!

In the end, the dentists won. Today, pretty much everyone agrees that (a) thumb sucking is harmful, and (b) it's usually an easy and nontraumatic habit to break. Finger sucking is a normal behavior in babies, seen in as many as 93 percent of one- and two-year-olds (in industrialized nations, anyway; in places where mothers have more contact with young children, interestingly, finger sucking is almost unheard of). And it's a perfectly harmless form of self-soothing until the age of four or so. That's when it can start leading to a variety of dental problems—most commonly an anterior overbite—but the full list includes everything from TMJ pains to speech impediments to a rare condition known as "having the mouth of Sloth from *The Goonies*."

The miracle cure for most thumb sucking is time: kids grow out of it, especially once they're around peers who don't suck. (Their thumbs, that is. Your kids' preschool friends *will* probably suck, in general.) If that doesn't happen, simple tools like positive reinforcement and distraction work well, since most thumb-suckers suck out of boredom. If there's anxiety underlying the habit, clearing up the causes of the anxiety usually puts the thumb back where it belongs. As a last resort, most dentists are okay with using a mouth appliance to correct the behavior. In the old days, this was an ominous contraption called a "hay-rake," which I like to imagine covered with pointy tines straight out of a medieval torture chamber. Today's "palatal cribs" sound far more comforting. Thumbs-up for euphemisms!

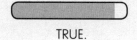

TRUE.

"You'll Eat It and You'll Like It!" (Mealtime Misinformation)

"Breakfast is the most important meal of the day!"

Or so my mom used to say, while forcing us to eat "a hot breakfast" every school morning, because apparently heating a Pop-Tart produces some crucial, health-imparting chemical change in its molecules. Taken literally, this parental maxim is silly. I know of no society on Earth where the morning meal is the most important meal of the day. For whatever reason, modern humans have been wired to center their eating—and plan their day—around lunch or dinner. And there are plenty of two-meal cultures in Eastern Europe, Asia, and Africa that eat no breakfast whatsoever, or at least a very minimal one.

But maybe the hyperbole is forgivable. The "most important meal" cliché, which dates back to the nineteenth century, serves as an attempt to overcompensate for breakfast's perennial also-ran status. Dinner doesn't need a press agent! Everyone will always eat dinner. But breakfast is often skipped, for lack of time or appetite or both. A 2011 market research survey found that 14 percent of teens skip breakfast. That number rises in young adulthood to 18 percent for women and a whopping 28 percent for men. So breakfast may at least be the most important meal of the day *relative to its perceived importance*.

The importance of breakfast is occasionally pooh-poohed by authors of fad diets emphasizing fasting or sleep advocates worried that getting kids up early for breakfast does harm to the circadian-rhythmically challenged. But with those exceptions, there's a broad scientific consensus that there are specific and unique benefits to eating breakfast. Most studies on breakfast and weight gain, for example, have found that breakfast-skippers are, counterintuitively, fatter than breakfast-eaters, perhaps because skipping a morning meal leads to less appetite control and bad dietary choices later in the day. A 2011 University of Minnesota study found a possible mechanism for this: their breakfast-eating subjects had healthier glucose levels as long as five hours later, which would reduce their risk of obesity and diabetes.

The health benefits of breakfast, particularly in children, aren't limited to body mass index. The blood-sugar-regulating effects of breakfast have also been shown to reduce the risk of diabetes and heart disease. And multiple investigations of students all over the world, from Japanese medical students to American middle schoolers, have found an increase in daytime fatigue in the breakfast-skippers, leading to lower cognitive function. A 2002 study of underperforming kids in inner-city Boston public schools found that introducing a free school-breakfast program boosted math scores, behavior marks, and attendance.

I'm an especially tragic case: a person who loves all breakfast food, from grapefruit to bacon to waffles to Cinnamon Toast Crunch, but who has literally no morning appetite. If you're like me in this regard, I've discovered that the best solution is a two-pronged approach: First, obtain a job that allows for bleary-eyed mornings surfing the Internet in lieu of any task requiring normal human blood-sugar levels. (Freelance writer is excellent for this.) Second, find a diner that serves all-day breakfast and doesn't judge customers who want pumpkin pancakes at, say, two in the afternoon or midnight. Voilà, an almost functional life. But I still make my kids eat breakfast.

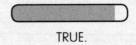

TRUE.

"It's okay, just pick it up and eat it. Five-second rule!"

School cafeteria lore may differ on the exact length of the grace period—sometimes it's the "three-second rule," sometimes it's as long as ten or fifteen seconds—but everyone agrees on the central truth in question: if you reach for a dropped fruit snack or piece of string cheese with sufficiently ninja-like speed, you can recover the endangered sweetmeat before noxious floor bacteria swarm all over it. This seems to be a relatively new idea in the annals of hygiene. Friends have told me they remember the five-second rule from the 1950s and 1960s, but it didn't become widespread until the 1990s (I first encountered it in college) and the first media references I can find to the "rule" date back only to the year 2000.

I'm not sure what mechanism proponents of the rule have in mind for its operation. Is the idea that food in free fall has some force field protecting it, one that stays intact for the first few seconds after impact? Or do we imagine that bacteria are so stunned by the new morsel ("Check it out, everybody! A Cheez-It the size of an aircraft carrier!") that they regard it with five seconds of awe before invading? We need wonder no longer, because the first generation raised on the five-second rule went off to college and began testing it out in labs. The pioneer in this field was Jillian Clarke, a high school intern at the University of Illinois who spent part of 2003 dropping Gummi Bears and fudge-stripe cookies onto *E. coli*–treated floor tiles. Microbes contaminated the food immediately, not after some magical five-second window. (This is what you'd expect: landing on the germs is what does the trick, not sitting around waiting for more to drift by.) Clarke won an Ig Nobel Prize for her groundbreaking work, and a team that followed up at Clemson University found similar results. In one of their tests, a piece of bologna dropped on germy tile managed to gather 99 percent of the bacteria in the first five seconds!

You may have read a dissenting opinion in 2007, when two

Connecticut College seniors tried a similar test with apple slices and Skittles in their dorm dining hall. Even when they left the food on the floor for 300 seconds, they found no bacteria transfer and therefore claimed they had not only validated the five-second rule but extended it to a new five-minute frontier! In fact, the Connecticut results were consistent with the earlier tests, which also found no contamination . . . unless the floor was pretreated with bacteria. It's true that most floors won't harbor *E. coli,* but some will—according to microbiologists, bacteria are perfectly capable of surviving on hard surfaces for weeks or even months. And there are plenty of other toxic things that your Fig Newton could pick up even from a germ-free floor—cleaning chemicals, for example, or bug spray.

Bottom line: most food can be retrieved from the floor after one second or one minute and you'd be just fine. But if there *was* something gross on the floor, the dropped food was equally gross before and after the five-second cutoff. In math terms: there is no "n-second rule" for any nonzero quantity n.

MOSTLY FALSE.

"Eat everything on your plate, there are children starving in Africa!"

Technically, yes, there are children starving in Africa. Even if your parents used China or India for this suppertime guilt trip, there are, sadly, lots of children starving there too. In 2009, UNICEF estimated that 195 million children were starving worldwide. Even in the United States, three million children suffer from hunger. You could say, "There are children starving in" pretty much any place on Earth and you'd be right. (Well, not Antarctica.)

The sentiment behind this awareness-raising platitude, however, is a little more specific. It's intended to make kids *feel guilty* for not finishing a meal, as if their lack of appetite is somehow contributing to problems of global food distribution. The idea dates back to the "Clean Plate Club" campaign dreamed up by the U.S. Food Administration (then headed by future president Herbert Hoover) in 1917, with the aim of using scarce supplies more efficiently during World War I and reducing food imports from overseas. Around the same time, the Ottoman Empire's genocide of its Armenian minority was becoming a cause célèbre in U.S. humanitarian circles, and every mom who read *Life* magazine began lecturing kids to finish their broccoli for "the starving Armenians." Future generations would update the saying to include Biafra, Ethiopia, or wherever the latest heart-tugging famine was located.

The problem with the "starving children!" guilt trip is that it's created a generation or two of Americans who feel it's somehow immoral to leave food uneaten. Unless you are in the elastic-waist jeans industry, you probably agree that juvenile obesity is a major problem today, and portion size is part of the reason. In 1955, the largest McDonald's hamburger patty was just 1.6 ounces; today, the chain's biggest burger has five times as much meat. Cereal eaters pour 20 percent more cornflakes and 30 percent more milk than they did just two decades ago. Even dinner plates had to get bigger in the early 1990s to account for our bigger appetites, ballooning from ten inches to twelve inches on average. A 2008 study at Cornell found that preschoolers who get pressured to finish meals at home requested larger servings of sugary day-care snacks as well. The study's authors suggest that food-"wasting" kids learn to listen to their body's fullness cues, whereas the "clean plate club" kids turn into overeaters, because they've learned to keep eating any time there's still food within reach of their pudgy little fingers.

Even worse, kids don't have to get very old before they realize that the correct answer to "There are children starving in China!" is to say, "Then why don't you send it to them?" in a sassy voice that gets them sent to their rooms and then Mommy needs an extra glass of wine or two before bed. Instead of insisting on the "clean plate club," it's much better to start with smaller servings and let kids decide if they want seconds or not. Then donate to the food bank or write a check to the Hunger Project instead of nagging the family about famine relief.

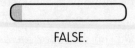

FALSE.

"Eat your crusts, that's where the vitamins are!"

For decades, parents have used this misinformation campaign to get kids to finish their bread. (Sometimes the crusts were also said to have magical powers to make your hair curly, apparently a much-desired physical attribute back in the day.) The reasons for the myth are murky—moms and dads trying not to waste food or tired of cutting the crusts off PB & J sandwiches? Or it might have been genuine confusion over the fact that many fruits and vegetables are, indeed, healthier with the peels on. In some cases, like potatoes, cooking with the peel intact keeps vitamins from leaching out into the surrounding water. In other cases, the outer part of a fruit might be inherently richer in fiber or nutrients than the inside. Apple peels, for example, have five times more polyphenol antioxidants than the rest of the fruit. Grape skins are the best source for cancer-preventing resveratrol. Health-food gurus even swear by hard-to-eat fruit wrappings like hairy kiwi skin (full of flavonoids and folic acid!) and banana peels (depression-fighting serotonin, cataract-preventing lutein!).

But bread, as you may be aware, is not a fruit. Bread crust is not some other form of plant tissue that's been stuck onto the outside of a loaf, like grape skins or a banana peel. The whole thing, crust and crumb, was shaped from exactly the same blob of dough, all parts of which contain exactly the same ingredients. It's just that one part got a little browner in the oven than the rest of it did. Vitamins don't migrate to the outside of a bread loaf while it's being baked, so there's nothing special about the crust.

Well, *almost* nothing. In 2002, some scientists at the German Research Center for Food Chemistry discovered, for the first time, that bread crust can have one nutritional advantage over the inside of the bread. The Maillard reaction, the same chemical change that makes browned food taste better than raw food, also creates an antioxidant called pronyl-lysine, which may have cancer-fighting potential. If bread is properly browned, the crust will be eight times richer in pronyl-lysine than the noncrust part of the bread—so your parents were right. (Sort of. Accidentally.) But Thomas Hofmann, the study's lead researcher, warns that overbrowning the crust reduces antioxidant levels, and burning it can even introduce carcinogens. You live by the crust, you die by the crust.

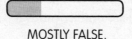

MOSTLY FALSE.

"No snacks, you'll ruin your dinner!"

I was a chronic between-meals foodnapper as a kid, so it's karmically correct that I should be the one who has to clean out the Hershey's Kiss wrappers and Goldfish cracker crumbs that mysteriously appear in my son's bedroom every time we vacuum or change his sheets. That's probably where parental disapproval of snacking comes from: the fact that many kids *will* binge unhealthily if the cookies aren't hidden cleverly enough. Well, that and the soul-killing experience of slaving away for hours over a hot stove to make dinner only to have the kids poke suspiciously at it because they filled up on Doritos earlier.

But there's nothing *inherently* unhealthy about snacking. Many nutritionists today recommend trying to eat six small meals a day instead of the traditional three large ones. Caloric intake, of course, is what matters most, but many people find it easier to avoid overeating at mealtimes if they keep their blood-sugar levels even all day with more frequent minimeals. It's a matter of preference.

A 2010 study at the University of North Carolina blames snacking for the recent weight gain in American kids. The average child in this country now eats 168 more calories' worth of snacks every day than in 1977, enough chips and granola bars to add 13.5 pounds of body fat per year. The $68-billion-a-year snack food industry ("Big Pretzel," I call them) is overjoyed about this development; dietitians, not so much. But, again, this doesn't mean all between-meals eating is a bad idea. Boredom snacking is a bad idea. Eating-only-Twinkies-because-they-taste-better-than-dinner is a bad idea. A healthy snack is fine. The right answer to "I need a snack" isn't "You'll ruin your dinner!" It's probably, "Sure, do you want an apple or a banana?" (Let's face it: when the options are that horrible, kids will probably save eating for dinnertime anyway.)

MOSTLY FALSE.

"Dinner is not a race! Chew each bite thirty times!"

If you have no idea how many times your kids chew each bite of food they eat, you are clearly the worst parent in the world. I just stealthily observed my daughter eating lunch and I'm pretty much the expert now, in case you have any questions. Her chewing seemed to me to fall somewhere in the healthy range between Cookie Monster and cow:

a dozen chews or so for a mouthful of something soft, like mac and cheese, but maybe twice that for something a little more challenging, like leftover chicken and broccoli from last night's Chinese.

Digestion starts in the mouth, thanks to both the food-crushing power of your teeth and the enzymes found in your saliva. So insufficient chewing can make life harder on your digestive tract. But unless kids are gulping down food whole with their head in the air, like a seagull working on a French fry, they're probably chewing enough to avoid an upset stomach. But could *more* chewing be even better? It probably could!

The sport of extreme chewing dates back to nineteenth-century American food faddist Horace Fletcher, who would spend hours "Fletcherizing" his food, which sounds filthy but consists only of chewing each bite one hundred times. His nationwide lectures on good chewing habits made him a millionaire, and his followers included Henry James, John D. Rockefeller, and Franz Kafka. He became nationally known as "the Great Masticator," which I bet, even in the Victorian era, teenagers thought was funny.

I must have less free time than Franz Kafka, because one hundred chews seems a bit much to me. I just tried it out with an apple and suppressing the swallow reflex was murder after forty or fifty. But scaled-down Fletcherism is still alive and well in modern health circles. To curb obesity, the Japanese government recently recommended that kids chew each bite thirty times, and there's plenty of evidence that this actually works. The chewing advice is mostly a crutch to slow down eating. Our stomach's "I'm full now!" signal can take as long as twenty minutes to reach the brain, so if you're eating slowly enough that meals last that long, you'll probably eat less. A 2011 study in China found that, in addition, the act of chewing creates a feeling of satiety by suppressing appetite-stimulating hormones and releasing appetite-suppressing ones. The forty-chews-per-bite group ate 12 percent fewer calories than the fifteen-chews-per-bite group.

I hate to sound like Yoda, but more chewing leads to more *mindfulness*: you'll enjoy your food more and probably eat healthier too. Dr. Fletcher knew what he was talking about. Of course, he also advocated studying your poop every day to make sure its color and odor were acceptable. I think that's carrying mindfulness a little too far.

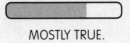

MOSTLY TRUE.

"No double-dipping, you'll spread germs!"

In a 1993 episode of the sitcom *Seinfeld,* Jerry's friend George Costanza commits yet another of the endless series of egregious social missteps that make up his miserable life. At the wake of his girlfriend's aunt, he dips a tortilla chip into a bowl of creamy dip, takes a bite, then dips again. An observant relative is scandalized, George is defiant ("You dip the way you want to dip, and I'll dip the way I want to dip!"), and yada yada yada, a fight breaks out. A new bit of hygiene awareness entered the American lexicon: the "double dip."

When Paul Dawson, a food science professor at Clemson University, caught a rerun of that episode in 2007, he got more than a catchphrase and a lesson in buffet-table etiquette: he got the idea for a scientific study. Dawson assembled a group of student volunteers, gave them each a bowl of dip and a box of Wheat Thins (ah, Wheat Thins, the lab rat of snack crackers), and instructed them to go to work—Costanza-style. After each cracker had been successively double-dipped, the leftover dip was cultured so that germs could be counted.

Would a quick bite, a millisecond on the teeth, really transplant germs from mouth to bowl? Dr. Dawson expected "little or no microbial transfer." He was shocked by the results: when a cracker was double-dipped three to six times, ten thousand new bacteria were introduced to their hummus-y new home. George was wrong and your mom was right: double-dipping is pretty disgusting. The study found that thicker dips were a little safer, because they mingled less with the bowl on each redip, and so were more acidic ones. But either way, between fifty and one hundred bacteria were moving from mouth to mouth with every bite. "Before you have some dip at a party," Dawson warned in *The New York Times,* "look around and ask yourself, would I be willing to kiss everyone here? Because you don't know who might be double dipping, and those who do are sharing their saliva with you."

The Clemson study is silent on my preferred double-dipping loop-hole as a child: to dip one end of my chip or crudité, take a bite, and then redip the *other,* untainted end. But even the unsanitary kind of double-dipping is more icky than dangerous. Most aerobic bacteria in the mouth are pretty harmless, so it's not as if there's going to be an outbreak of bubonic plague every time someone goes in for a second dose of salsa. After all, a form of double-dipping is the de facto method of eating in many other parts of the world, from the fondues of Switzer-land to the communal plates, open to the chopsticks of all, that make up a Japanese meal. Dr. Dawson is eager to test all these new international frontiers in social hygiene. In fact, he says he may even court religious protest by analyzing how much spit winds up in Communion wine.

Maybe then he can move on to other Costanza-inspired experi-ments in food hygiene. Like just how gross it is to eat a chocolate éclair out of a kitchen trash can. (Season six: "The Gymnast.")

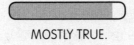

MOSTLY TRUE.

"Stay out of the cookie dough, you'll get worms!"

Worms? In cookie dough? This old chestnut clearly has its origins not in a research lab but from a frazzled mom tired of kids sticking their grubby fingers in a bowl of raw cookie dough. There are foods that can give you intestinal parasites, but pork products and undercooked shellfish are the most common culprits. Unless you use a lot of lobster roe or pork belly in your chocolate chip cookies, your dough is almost guaranteed to be worm-free.

Bacteria, of course, are another story. It's long been known that egg-shells can harbor salmonella, but in 1985, food-poisoning hysteria got kicked up another notch when scientists at the Centers for Disease Control were surprised to find salmonella lurking *inside* an egg's yolk membrane, from the salmonella-infested ovary of a perfectly healthy-seeming chicken. The FDA estimates that about one in every twenty thousand American eggs is contaminated. There are about three hundred million laying hens in the United States today—that's one hen, more or less, for every man, woman, and child. Good luck finding the few infected ones.

Since 1985, then, the FDA has taken a strong no-raw-eggs-*ever* stance, despite the fact that 53 percent of American college students admit to the occasional raw-dough sneaking. In a 2008 food safety podcast, an FDA scientist was asked about the practice. "It's really dangerous for children (or adults) to eat raw cookie dough, or lick the beaters after mixing batter containing raw eggs," she said.

Really dangerous? Er, no. That one-in-twenty-thousand number means that the average egg-consumer will come across a dangerous egg once every eighty-four years. It's true: if you're coming up on that one rare bad egg, *and* it was in the middle of the pallet so the bacteria multiplied before the egg got refrigerated, *and* that happens to be the one egg you're eating unpasteurized in cookie dough (or sunny-side up, or in homemade mayo, or whatever), you will get food poisoning. Here are the numbers: about a million Americans get salmonella every year, and twenty thousand get a bad enough case to send them to the hospital. About four hundred die, and a quarter of those are kids, with infants at the very highest risk.

But the egg kind of salmonella accounts for only 18 percent of all cases—poultry, for example, is much more dangerous. Salmonella bacteria are everywhere: in fast food, in your kitchen sponge, clinging to the outside of carefully washed fruits and vegetables. In 2009, the journal *Clinical Infectious Diseases* did publish evidence, for the first time, of a food-poisoning outbreak that originated with raw cookie dough. Thirty-five people were hospitalized in thirty different states after eating commercially sold dough. But here's the kicker: the culprit wasn't the eggs! "Raw flour is the only raw agricultural product that was in the cookie dough," said the study's epidemiologist. It was *E. coli* in the wheat flour that laid out the dough-snatchers, not salmonella in the eggs! What are you going to do, stop dusting flour on stuff?

The moral, I suppose, is that everything in life is a risk. Lightning kills about as many people a year as egg-borne salmonella, and there are some lightning precautions we think make sense (don't hold a five-iron aloft as thunder booms above the golf course) and some that don't (never go outside if there are clouds). To my mind, licking the beater and/or mixing bowl when Mom or Dad makes cookies is one of the purest joys of childhood, and maybe even worth the once-every-eighty-four-years case of food poisoning. Same goes for sunny-side-up eggs and homemade aioli, come to think of it. Sorry, FDA.

If you *are* a purist about raw eggs and don't hate your children enough to withhold the beater, remember that there are safer alternatives for cookie dough that little mouths might be sampling. Grocery stores sell pasteurized eggs now, or you can use any number of nonegg substitutes when you bake. Lots of people swear by flaxseed, for example. So there's no reason to traumatize kids, parents: let them lick that bowl and then they won't grow up to hate you and become serial killers.

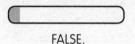

FALSE.

"Stop opening the door and peeking in the oven! All the heat goes out!"

I heard this every time I opened the oven door as a child to see if the cookies were done yet. (Baking a batch of cookies is the best way to slow down time for children, with the possible exception of cooling freshly baked cookies on a cookie rack.) Utility companies and energy commissions agree with Mom: oven peeking is a big heat-saving no-no, they say, like you might as well be wrapping a six-pack ring around a sea turtle's beautiful neck every time you check on your lasagna or layer cake. The scary statistic often cited is 25 percent: an oven can lose a full quarter of its heat during a single peek.

In his 1992 book *The Curious Cook,* bestselling kitchen-science writer Harold McGee tried this out. He was able to get oven temperature to drop by a quarter or more, from 450° down to 350°, but only by leaving the door open for a full minute. That's not an unreasonable amount of time to spend basting a turkey or checking on a roast, but it's still longer than a kid's peek would last. More to the point, McGee was surprised to find that the temperature bounced back fully in less than a minute! He was using a gas oven, and found that the lost heat magically reappeared without a burner even igniting. How is this possible? Because most of an oven's heat is radiated from its walls. The air around your pan gets slightly cooler when the door's open, but the walls don't, and they're storing enough heat to make up for the loss. "Different ovens behave differently," says McGee, "but I'll bet that most cooks can afford to relax."

Very delicate dishes like soufflés can be finicky about temperature changes. But almost any other food will be just fine, no matter how antsy the kids get. Watched pots still boil, and watched cookies still bake.

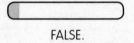

FALSE.

"Sugar rots your teeth!"

The old saw about sugar rotting your teeth seems obviously true. But if you look a little closer, you realize it's technically false. Learn a little more about the chemistry involved and it starts to look true again. Then look at the research and it looks more false. It's like Schrodinger's Dental Cliché.

Here's the sweet science: sugar itself doesn't do any harm to tooth enamel. The problem is that your mouth is full of bacteria that thrive on carbohydrates, including sugars. When they get carbs, they break them down into by-products that include acids, and it's the resulting *acid,* not the sugar, that eats away at your teeth. So sugar doesn't rot teeth—but that's a technicality, like "Guns don't kill people." Effectively it does, by feeding bacteria.

But wait. If your mouth microbes can turn any carbohydrate into acid, is there anything special about sugar? The answer is no. Bread, rice, many fruits and vegetables—all are starchy enough to keep the bacteria on your teeth drilling cavities for hours. You could eat a strict no-sugar diet, and if you didn't brush and floss regularly, you'd still have the mouth of a Dickensian orphan. I suppose it's plausible that sugars would be worse than other carbs because they're stickier, but it turns out that's not true either. In the 1990s, a New York University dental researcher named Harold Linke conducted a series of tests on the staying power of different kinds of dental plaque, and cooked starches were much worse than sugars. Your saliva is pretty good at washing away the remnants of a candy bar but not so hot when it comes to potato chips ground into molars.

So why do dentists hate on sugar so much? Partially because of its other unredeeming qualities, like its connection to childhood obesity. (Although starchy snacks like potato chips don't look so great in that light either.) But mostly it's a matter of timing. We do most of our carb loading at mealtimes and hopefully remember to brush afterward. But we tend to indulge our sugar habits between meals: a soda pop here, a tube of Rolos there. Hours might go by before a toothbrush interrupts the beautiful relationship between your afternoon snack and your smile. Cavities aren't so much a result of what you eat but of how long you leave it sitting there.

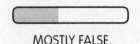

MOSTLY FALSE.

"Finish Your Milk!" (And Other Drinking Problems)

"You need eight glasses of water every day!"

This was called the "8 x 8 rule" when I heard about it from my seventh-grade home ec teacher, Mrs. Brown, who insisted that we should be drinking eight eight-ounce glasses of water every 24 hours. Couldn't be milk, couldn't be juice, couldn't be anything but water. I protested that surely all beverages were mostly water, and couldn't they therefore—? "No!"

Mrs. Brown was an older woman who has presumably passed from this life now—hopefully not in any ironic way, like drowning, because that would be terrible. But she has been outlived by the myth she helped propagate: that most people are probably dehydrated, because they're drinking some normal-seeming amount of water and not a superhuman-effort amount, like eight to ten glasses. This rule of thumb has been recommended by sensible nutritionists and water-will-cure-anything crackpots alike, but it's all wet.

In 2002, a Dartmouth physiology professor and kidney specialist named Heinz Valtin studied the myth for the *American Journal of Physiology* and concluded that the "rule" wasn't just a lie, it was an accident. In 1945, the Food and Nutrition Board of the National Research Council recommended "one milliliter of water for each calorie of food" eaten. A nineteen-hundred-calorie diet would indeed work out to about sixty-four ounces of water a day. But, in typical American short-attention-span fashion, everyone appears to have forgotten the very next sentence: "Most of this quantity is contained in prepared foods." That's right, Mrs. Brown: most of our water gets to us in non-water form. In fact, a National Institutes of Health doctor told the *Los Angeles Times* in 2000 that a healthy adult in a temperate climate could probably replace his body's daily water loss on food alone, without a single glass of water!

Dr. Valtin says that, unless you have kidney stones or a urinary tract infection or something, you should probably worry more about drinking too much water than not enough. Athletes and fad-dieters occasionally get something called "water intoxication," where their electrolytes get so watered down that their brain goes wonky. Anthony Andrews, the British actor you might remember from *Brideshead Revisited* or *The Scarlet Pimpernel,* spent three days in intensive care in 2003 when he drank too much water during an exhausting run playing Henry Higgins in *My Fair Lady* in the West End. (I guess the rain in Spain stayed mainly in his brain.) Andrews recovered, but others haven't been so lucky; overhydration can be fatal. Dr. Valtin also points out that drinking too much water can be time-consuming and embarrassing (all those pee breaks!), not to mention expensive and ecologically iffy (if you choose bottled water).

So what is the right amount of water to drink? Whatever your body tells you to, by this weird mechanism called "being thirsty." You start to feel thirsty when the concentration of your blood goes up less than 2 percent, and that's plenty of warning since dehydration doesn't start until you hit 5 percent or so. Don't count glasses, don't fixate on urine color. Just go get a drink when you feel thirsty. And it doesn't have to be water: a 2000 study by the Center for Human Nutrition found that even supposedly "diuretic" beverages like coffee, tea, and caffeinated soda provide almost all of the hydration that water does. I'm just glad Mrs. Brown didn't live to see this day.

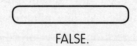

FALSE.

"I can hear your heart racing from here," observes Calvin's pet tiger Hobbes as the comic strip menace dives into a second bowl of Chocolate Frosted Crunchy Sugar Bombs. "They make these with marshmallow bits, too, but Mom won't buy them for me," replies Calvin.

It's the myth of the "sugar high"—the idea that sugary candy, sodas, and cereals cause kids to bounce off the walls like little SuperBalls. This dates back to the Feingold Diet of the 1970s, in which California allergist Ben Feingold first recommended treating hyperactivity in children by avoiding food additives like artificial colors and sweeteners. Feingold didn't ban all sugar, but it became a popular target for parental crackdowns anyway.

Dozens of recent studies, however, have soured doctors on the possible linkage. Sugar doesn't really wind kids up, they now believe—it's just that many of the occasions on which kids eat lots of sugar, like birthday parties and holidays, tend to be chaotic anyway. A revealing 1994 experiment by Daniel Hoover and Richard Milich put the blame for this myth squarely on the parents' shoulders: they showed that moms and dads were much more likely to classify their kids' behavior as hyper when told that the kids had just gotten buzzed on sugar. (In reality, all the kids in the study were drinking a sugar-free placebo.)

Cutting down on sugar is great for kids' teeth and weight, of course. It just won't help them sit still longer in a third-grade classroom or on Grandma's plastic-covered couch or at a crowded chain restaurant. Some research has even found that sugar has a calming effect on younger kids. Maybe Calvin just needed a *third* bowl of Chocolate Frosted Crunchy Sugar Bombs to settle down that racing heartbeat.

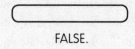

FALSE.

"Coffee will stunt your growth!"

In the nineteenth century, one of the most common warnings made against the evils of tobacco was that it would "stunt the growth of both body and mind" in young boys who smoked. There's probably some truth to this: a 2008 study by the Canadian Cancer Society found that teens who smoked were, on average, an inch shorter than their cleaner-lunged classmates. But by the 1930s, the growth-stunting meme had spread to a less pernicious adult vice, the morning cup of joe, and coffee companies were forced to launch ad campaigns to combat these "old-time fears and prejudices."

There is, in fact, no evidence linking coffee drinking to growth problems. Some of these worries may stem from another parental canard, the one about carbonated drinks being bad for your bones. When studies showed that only colas, and not other carbonated drinks, were linked to lower bone density and osteoporosis, suspicion shifted to caffeine. Could caffeine really make kids shorter after all, by limiting their bone growth? A 2001 study by Creighton University researchers found that the answer was no: caffeinated drinks do cause a small calcium deficiency, but over a twenty-four-hour period, the body is quite efficient at making up the difference by flushing out less calcium when you pee. "The net effect of carbonated beverage constituents on calcium economy is negligible," wrote the authors. So how do we explain the evidence that Coke is worse for your bones than Sprite is? A 2006 Tufts study suggested that the culprit might be phosphoric acid, a common cola ingredient that raises the acidity of your blood. The body may be releasing calcium ions from your bones to help neutralize the acid.

But caffeine seems to be off the hook. Medical debunkers Aaron Carroll and Rachel Vreeman point out that caffeine has been used in neonatal wards since the 1970s, to alleviate apnea and other breathing problems in premature infants. If growth problems were a side effect, we probably would have noticed by now. It's been suggested that coffee's rap as a growth stunter might come down to secondary behavioral factors—coffee drinkers getting less sleep or drinking less milk—rather than physiological ones. Now, coffee can produce side effects in kids, like irritability and sleeplessness, that I wouldn't wish on my worst parental enemy. My kids are certainly enough of a handful even without a Starbucks grande Americano in their system. But rest assured that even if coffee gets your kids nice and wired, it won't make *them* any shorter. Just your temper.

FALSE.

"It's too hot for milk, it'll curdle in your stomach!"

I've heard several versions of this bizarre warning over the years: don't drink milk when you exercise, don't drink milk with orange juice, don't drink milk when you have a fever. But in all cases, the alleged health risk is the same: the otherwise nutritious dairy product will curdle inside you, upsetting your stomach.

This old-timey warning may originate from those unpleasant cases when parents and kids got a second look at a glass of milk they'd drunk earlier, in the form of throw-up. The milk certainly looked curdled, thus proving the folk wisdom. But, as you've probably heard, your stomach juices contain hydrochloric acid, one of the strongest acids known. As a result, milk begins to curdle within seconds of reaching your stomach, even when you're perfectly healthy. It's just that we only get to see evidence of the curdling when you're *not* feeling so hot. Non-cultured dairy products have been known to aggravate cases of gastroenteritis, so milk isn't the best thing for an upset stomach. But if you're feeling good, there's nothing wrong with a cool glass of it on a hot day.

No one has done more to prop up the misconceptions about

milk's being dangerous in combination with heat and/or fruit than nineteenth-century Whig president Zachary Taylor. On the morning of July 4, 1850, President Taylor attended a fund-raiser for the still-unfinished Washington Monument. It was a swelteringly hot day, and when the president got back to the White House, he loaded up on cold milk and cherries to cool off. Within five days, he was dead of a vicious digestive illness. Today we suspect the bug that killed him was dysentery or something along those lines, but nineteenth-century writers always played up a fatal connection between the milk and cherries and heat, which may have helped cement this myth in the public mind.

Some historians, incidentally, have long believed that Zachary Taylor's death was no accident, but that someone spiked his cherries with arsenic. The nation was facing a crucial secessionist crisis at the time of his death, and it's very possible that the following decade and U.S. Civil War would have unfolded very differently had he lived. Taylor's remains were even dug up and analyzed in 1991, but no unusual traces of arsenic were found. The notion is still kicking around today, though, since conspiracy theorists are rarely discouraged by actual facts. I guess we'll have to wait for the inevitable Oliver Stone film adaptation to settle the matter.

FALSE.

"Quit shaking your pop cans, you'll make a mess!"

In my family, soda explosions were taken deadly seriously. Any shaken can of Shasta, or one that had gotten loose and rolled around the back of the station wagon for an hour, was treated like a hand grenade. We weren't allowed to drink it for hours, and even then it had to be opened gingerly, as if by one of the unexploded-bomb experts from *The Hurt Locker*.

Now that I have kids, I understand the caution, of course. It only takes one cleanup of gooey Coke residue from a coffee table or car interior to give any parent post-traumatic stress disorder about future can openings. Using my wife's laptop is still a weird, sticky-clicky experience thanks to the can of root beer my son spilled on the keyboard a couple of months back. But all this concern is unnecessary nowadays. Not too many people seem aware of the fact, but aluminum soda cans just don't explode anymore.

The kids and I just headed out to the backyard with a six-pack of cola and a six-pack of diet cola, both slightly chilled. (Sitting-in-an-unheated-garage chilled, not refrigerator-chilled. Our goal was to re-create the average picnic scenario.) We shook the cans vigorously for thirty seconds, then waited a brief interval, then opened them quickly. At five seconds, we found, the cans would still spatter and foam over. (The umbrella my five-year-old brought outside came in handy.) But somewhere between the ten- and fifteen-second marks, the foam stopped rising over the lip of the can. By twenty seconds, there was no reaction whatsoever, as if the can had never been shaken up at all.

I first learned the overhyped nature of soda explosions fifteen years ago, when I saw the magic duo Penn & Teller use it to do a nifty TV trick with two soda cans: the shaken can would "magically" do nothing, while the unshaken one would explode all over an unlucky Conan O'Brien or Keith Olbermann or whoever the interviewer was. Making the unshaken can explode, it turns out, is easy: you just give the aluminum a covert squeeze as you pop the top. But calming the shaken can was even easier: the magicians just needed to wait a few seconds. The audience apparently had no idea how easy that part was, judging by their gasps of astonishment.

Penn & Teller had no explanation for the fizz-iology of the trick, which they learned from fellow magician Paul Harris. "I guess they've changed the way they package soda or something," they offered. Maybe there's more head space or less carbonation or something in today's soda cans; I'm not sure. But I think it's more likely that soda *never* foamed all that much, and people are just gun-shy based on one bad experience with a just-shaken Coke, or one on a hot day (warm liquids hold less gas than cold ones), or one actively sprayed on them by a mischievous kid, or a bottle of beer or champagne.

The magical fifteen-second "refractory period" of carbonated beverages does explain another age-old misconception: the tapping-the-top-of-the-can ritual. Spokespeople for Coke and Pepsi have both disavowed the practice; so have chemistry and physics professors and professional myth-debunkers like Snopes.com, Cecil Adams, and the *MythBusters* team. And yet still it persists! The reason is simple: taking a few seconds to gently tap on a can delays your opening of it by a few seconds. Often, that time interval is all it takes to keep the can from spilling over. Whether you tap or don't, your pop is probably not going to pop.

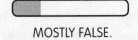

MOSTLY FALSE.

"Don't chew your ice, it's bad for your teeth!"

The chewing of ice is called pagophagia, a word undoubtedly chosen by science because it's almost as ugly and irritating as the noise of ice-chewing itself. But how is it that this sound—one that can inspire panic, fury, and occasionally homicide when it comes from the Big Gulp fan in the next cubicle—can also be strangely satisfying and even soothing when amplified a hundredfold and coming from inside your own head? Ah, sweet mystery of life!

Parents are on solid dental ground when they insist that kids cut it out with the iceberg-calving racket that is ice-chewing. Ice cubes are a perfect storm of two things that are terrible for your enamel: hard surfaces and rapid temperature change. The cold makes your tooth fibers contract just as you're smashing them with, in effect, a big rock-hard piece of crystal. Most of the time you'll be fine, but if you hit that sucker just wrong, you'll chip off a big chunk of your tooth.

That said, children are probably the world's safest candidates for ice-chewing. The teeth that chip on ice are most often those that were already weakened by age, previous microfractures, or fillings, and children's teeth don't usually qualify. Kids who still have their baby teeth should care even less, but kids with braces should be even more careful due to the possibility of breaking a bracket or screwing up wires.

Parents should be aware that ice-chewing is also a common symptom of iron-deficiency anemia. A 1968 study from the *Annals of Internal Medicine* found that over 60 percent of its sample size of anemics reported pagophagia among their symptoms. In all but one case, the ice-chewing went away when the anemia was treated. No one is quite sure why an iron deficiency should make you want to chew on ice, but it might be because it numbs the mouth pain that's another common symptom of anemia. Only a doctor can tell if your little ice-chomper is anemic (try iron pills) or just annoying (try noise-canceling headphones).

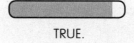

TRUE.

"I Told You to Go Before We Left the House!"
(Bathroom Badgering)

> ## "Put down the lid before you flush! You're spreading bacteria everywhere!"

If you heard this warning from a germophobe parent, you have one man to thank: Dr. Charles Gerba, an environmental microbiologist at the University of Arizona. Gerba is *the* man to call when you have a tricky question about bacteria and/or bathrooms, having written over four hundred journal articles on fecal filth and consulted on toilet problems everywhere from Antarctica (the National Science Foundation's McMurdo Station) to deep space (educating both NASA and the Russians on space-station sanitation). He even gave his oldest son the middle name Escherichia, which is the "E" in "E. coli." (It was going to be Salmonella for a girl, he says.) He made an end run around his wife's family by telling them Escherichia was a little-known biblical king.

In the early 1970s, Gerba was studying viruses at Baylor University when his adviser pulled him into a restroom stall one fateful day and told him to drop his drawers. (Wait, this is not the kind of story you think.) When Gerba flushed, his adviser excitedly grabbed his knee. (Still not that kind of story.) "Did you feel that?" he asked. "The aerosol, the droplets! This is how viral disease spreads."

No one had ever studied the aerosol effects of flushing before, so Gerba went to work, inventing a strobe-light gadget to photograph a toilet's usually invisible fecal fountain and a "commodograph" to plot where the water would land. The results were shocking. "Droplets are going all over the place—it's like the Fourth of July," said Gerba. (You can duplicate his results by putting dye in your toilet bowl at home and then holding up a piece of typing paper during a flush.) Gerba advises flushing with the lid down, keeping your toothbrush in a medicine cabinet, and getting out of the bathroom as soon as you wash your hands, because once the poop hits the fan, it stays airborne for at least two hours.

When the hosts of TV's *MythBusters* tested this proposition in 2004, they were surprised to find fecal coliform bacteria in *all* their toothbrushes, even the control ones kept in a different room! This is consistent with much of Dr. Gerba's subsequent research, which seems to have been aimed at making every man, woman, and child in America into a pathological Howard Hughes–style OCD case. In 1998, for example, he found that the toilet seat was actually one of the least germy parts of the house, much cleaner than your kitchen sponge, cutting board, or sink. "If an alien came from space and studied the bacterial counts," said the eminently quotable scientist, "he probably would conclude he should wash his hands in your toilet and crap in your sink." Or possibly on your desk at work: in 2001, Gerba took on the workplace and found that literally every spot he tested—phone receivers, keyboards, photocopiers, elevator buttons—had more bacteria per square inch than the restroom toilet seat that everyone so uncomfortably hovers over. Your desktop at the office probably has four hundred times the bacteria the toilet does, because it's used more and cleaned less frequently, so you might want to start taking your Quiznos into the stall with you for lunch.

These findings are daunting, but don't put on your surgical mask and start bottling your urine just yet. Most of the millions of bacteria in Dr. Gerba's counts are totally harmless, and the majority of disease-causing germs can't survive on inanimate objects for long (cold and flu would be lucky to last half an hour on a door handle), so transmission is typically person-to-person. Still, most of the hardier food-borne illnesses are caught at home, so Dr. Gerba recommends regular bleach wipe-downs for sinks, countertops, faucet handles, and toilets. And, yes, put the lid down *before* you flush, rather than after (ladies) or never (guys).

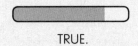

TRUE.

"Wash your hands after you use the bathroom!"

After reading the research in the previous entry, in which toilet seats were held up as paragons of spotless purity compared to the cesspool that is the sink, you might be forgiven for wondering: in that case, why do I wash my hands after I go to the can? Isn't that just loading up on new microbes to take with me?

It's true that bathroom sinks, particularly in public restrooms, can be bacteria farms, because of all the just-went-to-the-bathroom people who congregate there. You certainly don't want to touch the surfaces there more than necessary. But just because sinks are grodier than toilet seats (because toilet seats stay drier, mostly) doesn't mean they're not cleaner than all the other, uh, surfaces you touch during your whole bathroom process. (Whatever that may be. Not my business.) As a result, doctors call hand-washing the single most important thing you can do to avoid illness. The World Health Organization estimates that frequent hand-washing reduces your chances of respiratory disease by 24 percent and cuts in half your chances of contracting a stomach bug.

But only if you do it right! When Americans are asked in surveys, 92 percent claim to be hand-washers, but when researchers actually stake out public restrooms, the number is closer to 83 percent. And even the people who do stop by the sink make a fairly half-assed attempt. (This is a scientific term, because they leave literally half the ass still on their hands.) A thorough hand-washing takes twenty seconds of vigorous soap-scrubbing, say the bacteria-counters, and two-thirds of us don't even use soap. Our average scrub time: eleven seconds. If you make one of these token "Don't judge me!" attempts at hand-washing at a public restroom sink, you're probably just making things worse: you've chosen to hang out at the grossest place in the room, and you're not even going to wash well while you're there dipping your hands in the microbial cocktail.

A 2008 study from a London university found that there's a wrong way to dry your hands as well. Those electric warm-air dryers actually doubled the number of bacteria on subjects' hands in the drying process, and the newfangled jet-air ones, the ones that can supposedly blow air on your hands at four hundred miles per hour, were capable of spreading the germs from your hands in a two-meter radius around the dryer. Good old-fashioned paper towels, by contrast, wiped away about 76 percent of the remaining bacteria and didn't spread a thing. (Don't feel too guilty about the environmental impact of paper towels. A 2002 report from Franklin Associates found that the use of a single paper towel had essentially the same carbon footprint as thirty seconds under a 2,400-watt dryer. More efficient dryers and/or recycled paper towels will change the math slightly, but any difference will be small.)

There is one time when a good, thorough hand-washing has been proved to be harmful: when the soap dispenser itself is full of contaminated soap. A 2011 study by an Ohio-based soap company found stomach-churning results: elementary-school soap dispensers that had literally never been cleaned, fuzzy molds growing on bar soap, and liquid-soap bacteria levels ten thousand times the normal range—as high as ten million microbes per milliliter. But public health officials say the solution isn't to stop washing your hands or to switch to Purell—instead, public restrooms just need to switch to the same kinds of sealed soap dispensers that hospitals use. Problem solved.

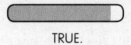

TRUE.

"Light a match in there, it'll get rid of the smell!"

This answer depends on your definition of "smell." Is it defined by the presence of odor molecules in the air, or is it in the nostril of the beholder? In other words, if a bear poops in the woods but there's no one there to smell it, does it still stink?

Tragically, there has been no academic work on this burning subject—which is odd, given the proximity of most universities to fraternity houses. Frats, it's well-known, consume half of the world's match supply every year in the name of making bathrooms enterable. You might be tempted to assume that the flame from your match is actually burning the stinkier components of bathroom odor into something more inert, smell-wise. After all, anyone who's spent any time with teenagers knows that flatus (the gas produced in farts) is a highly flammable substance. Columnist Cecil Adams reports the case of a Minnesota patient who was having a rectal polyp cauterized when a stray spark from the procedure ignited his intestinal gases, propelling the surgeon back into a wall and blowing a six-inch hole in the patient's gut. (Both recovered.) But I'm skeptical that the combustibility of farts explains the power of the bathroom match. Surely a lit match only burns air in the immediate vicinity of the flame and can't consume the smell in every far corner of the room.

John Christie, an Australian chemistry professor tackling this problem for the online MadSci Network, speculated that the plume of sulfur dioxide produced when a match head ignites is responsible. Sulfur dioxide has such a pungent smell that it effectively overpowers the nose, making other smells harder to detect for a period of time. In other words, the match might only mask the bathroom scent, not vanquish it for good.

The only real-world test of Dr. Christie's hypothesis that I know of was performed in 2006 by TV's *MythBusters*. They released the smelly stuff in human flatus—hydrogen sulfide and methyl mercaptan—into an airtight chamber and then lit a match. The concentration of those gases didn't go down, but a human judge did note a small decrease in the perceived smell of the methyl mercaptan, though not the hydrogen sulfide. In other words, the match smell had a mild masking effect on one component of bathroom stench, though the offending odor was still lurking there, and just as smelly as ever.

So it *is* slightly better to light a single candle than to curse the stinkiness. The smell won't go away, but at least it might get covered up for a while. My wife is a big fan of scented candles, so our bathroom never smells like poop. Instead, it smells like Caramel Apple Toffee and Poop, Lemongrass and Poop, or, every December, Christmas Memories and Poop. Mouthwatering!

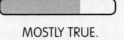

MOSTLY TRUE.

"Give your teeth a good hard brushing!"

"Good" is good, but "hard" is not so good. The consequences of not brushing your teeth well are widely known: cavities, gingivitis, bad breath. But dentists have known for over sixty years that you *can* have too much of a good thing: there are consequences to overbrushing as well. "Toothbrush abrasion"—damage to the enamel and gums caused by overly vigorous brushing—is widespread. In one Swedish study, 60 percent of teens already had gum damage from tooth brushing, and those numbers just got worse with age. Dentists say that we're brushing our teeth too hard, in the wrong direction, with the wrong toothbrush and too much toothpaste. In effect, despite having brushed our teeth maybe twice a day for the entire span of our lives, we're terrible at it.

Instead of scrubbing at your teeth as hard as you can, try brushing much more gently for more time—as long as two or three minutes is fine, most dentists say. Take a look at your toothbrush before the next time you brush. If the bristles flare outward, you're using too much pressure. A broad horizontal stroke along the front of your incisors may be the classic "I'm brushing my teeth!" pantomime motion, but it's been shown to cause two or three times more damage to tooth dentin than a vertical stroke. Smaller, circular motions will give you the best of both worlds while protecting your gums. Make sure you're not just focusing your brushing on one part of your mouth and neglecting others, a common bad-brushing habit that can lead to abrasion *and* cavities. Brushing twice a day is fine; most dentists say that brushing more often will do more harm than good. If you need still more detail on brushing methodology, a little research will produce any number of step-by-step daily regimens: the Bass method, the Charters, the Modified Stillman, the Rolling Stroke, the Modified Scrub. A veritable kama sutra of toothbrush techniques!

Dentists have long recommended a soft-bristled toothbrush to avoid beating up your gums, but there's still some scientific controversy on this point. A 2000 dental study from Bristol, England, discovered that softer bristles actually wore away *more* tooth enamel than firmer ones, probably because softer bristles hold toothpaste better. The British scientists hastened to add that the difference is small enough that nobody should risk gum disease by rushing out to buy a stiffer toothbrush, but the results do demonstrate that no toothbrush selection—not even a power or sonic toothbrush—is going to protect you 100 percent from abrasion problems. It's all in how you use it.

In April 1999, a suburban Chicago man named Mark Trimarco filed a class-action suit against the American Dental Association and eight toothbrush manufacturers, seeking damages for all those poor souls who had suffered toothbrush abrasion during the dental industry's fifty-year cover-up. Toothbrushes are "unreasonably dangerous," claimed the suit, and therefore should come with warning labels, like cigarettes. Trimarco's website featured the shocking news that toothbrush abrasion "is most prevalent in . . . people who brush their teeth" and, in fact, that "there are studies that show that people who do not brush their teeth, never develop" the symptoms! A soft-bristled judge dismissed the case the following year.

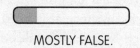

MOSTLY FALSE.

"Don't swallow your toothpaste, it's bad for you!"

It's a minor miracle that, in our litigious, overnannied society, toothbrushes still don't come with warning labels. But toothpaste does! In April 1997, the U.S. Food and Drug Administration ruled that toothpaste manufacturers weren't adhering closely enough to voluntary safety guidelines. As a result, all toothpaste tubes now bear a scary-sounding warning like this one: "Keep out of the reach of children under 6 years of age. If more than used for brushing is accidentally swallowed, get medical help or contact a Poison Control Center right away."

Emergency medical help right away? For swallowing *toothpaste*? In the months following the new warning, toothpaste consumer lines fielded hundreds of questions from worried parents, and poison control centers were flooded with calls as well. They told parents the same thing: your child is fine and may barf, or not. The only reason to see a doctor is if the vomiting gets so serious that dehydration becomes an issue. That's right: you can eat your fill of delicious, delicious toothpaste and not come away with anything more serious than nausea and diarrhea. The year before the warning label was put in place, 4,453 cases of "fluoride exposure" were reported to poison-control centers, but not a single one was life-threatening.

Make no mistake: fluoride salts are toxic in sufficient quantities, a fact that antifluoridation crackpots make much of. But a lethal dose of sodium fluoride for an adult is about five to ten grams. The family-sized tube of Colgate I just grabbed from the kids' bathroom holds eight ounces of toothpaste and less than half a gram of sodium fluoride. So I'd have to suck down more than a half gallon of the stuff to get into the lethal range. Kids weigh less than me, so they could get themselves sick with smaller doses, but they'd still have to finish off multiple tubes to do any serious damage.

So why the warning label? The American Dental Association's biggest concern about toothpaste—and the only side effect of fluoridation ever confirmed by actual case-control studies—is dental fluorosis, a cosmetic discoloration of the teeth that's not uncommon in kids who drink fluoridated water (about one in six get it). These little white specks are almost always harmless, but they'll get worse if kids snack on toothpaste, so the ADA has long recommended using just a pea-sized amount on the brush (just a smear for kids under three) and supervising the brushing of young children. The organization opposed the new government label, saying that it "greatly overstates any demonstrated or potential danger posed by fluoride toothpastes."

So it's a good idea to remind kids not to swallow their toothpaste, no matter how much they love the taste of mint and sorbitol. But don't feel bad if you don't get as worked up about the risk as your toothpaste tube label does.

MOSTLY TRUE.

"Make sure you shampoo every day!"

My mom counted herself lucky if we washed our hair once a week (usually on Saturday night, *Little House on the Prairie*–style!), but today more and more people lather up with shampoo daily. In turn-of-the-century America, the average hair-washing frequency was once a month—not that modern detergent-based shampoos had even been invented yet. The earliest "shampoos" were soap-based scalp massages prepared by hair salons. (The word "shampoo" even comes from the Hindi *champo,* meaning "to massage.") But in May 1908, a *New York Times* beauty column recommended shampooing *twice* as often, every two weeks! This kicked off a century-long arms race of escalating hair-washing frequency. Today, according to a Procter & Gamble survey,

Americans wash their hair 4.59 times every week, twice as often as people do in Spain or Italy.

Most dermatologists and stylists say that's too often. "Hair is a fiber," one dermatologist and hair research specialist told WebMD. "Think of a wool fiber: the more you wash it, the worse it's going to look. There's no need to wash your hair every day." The right frequency is going to vary based on your hair type and style, as well as by the type of shampoo you use, but two or three times a week is the average that doctors recommend. The oil-producing sebaceous glands in your scalp learn to compensate for your hair-care routine. If you're stripping away sebum (one of the few bodily secretions *less* gross than its name, by the way—it's just hair oil) on a daily basis, your body will just compensate by making more.

Shampoo companies, of course, want you to wash your hair every day. That way they move more product. A 2005 Dove study aimed at persuading women to lather up more revealed the shocking fact that 60 percent of women don't shampoo every day, in hopes of protecting their hair! Scandalous. On the other side of the spectrum is the "No 'Poo" movement, which cuts out commercial shampoos altogether (mostly to avoid additives like sulfates) in favor of a more natural approach, like baking soda and vinegar rinses. (If you combine the two, you get the look that salon stylists refer to as "science fair volcano.")

If you must shampoo the full 365 times a year, dermatologists recommend sticking to a lightweight shampoo marked for everyday use. And *don't* listen for the squeak of freshly rinsed hair as a sign of cleanliness, a noise my mom always insisted on. Hair only squeaks for two reasons: when you've washed it too much (and stripped it of so much natural oil that it might turn brittle and dry) or way too little (and there's a family of mice living in it).

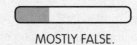

MOSTLY FALSE.

"Pee on your athlete's foot in the shower!"

Urine has been a home remedy for the fungal infection tinea pedis, or athlete's foot, for many years. It's widely available, it's cheap, and you don't have to worry about other family members stealing your supply. Peeing on foot infections got a big PR boost in 1994, when Madonna touted the cure in a Letterman interview. But I can't really recommend the same cure she used. That's super-gross. *Do not ask Madonna to pee on your feet!*

Peeing on your own feet, sadly, is just as ineffective. This myth has probably been reinforced by the fact that many commercial athlete's-foot creams do contain urea, the major solid component of human urine. Urea is how the body gets rid of excess nitrogen; it also has antimicrobial properties and softens and exfoliates skin. But there's just not enough of it in your pee to clear up athlete's foot. Some antifungal preparations are as much as 40 percent urea, twenty times the concentration of urine. And if you're trying out this remedy in the shower (the Madonna method) rather than soaking your feet in buckets of pee (Lady Gaga, probably), the shower will dilute and drain away the urea almost immediately.

I hasten to add that peeing on your feet in the shower doesn't do any harm either, since urine is nontoxic and perfectly sterile. A 2009 *Glamour* magazine poll found that 75 percent of women cop to peeing in the shower, so you can't even say it's a gross guy thing anymore. You might even save the planet. A Rio de Janeiro "save the rainforest" group ran a 2009 ad campaign to persuade Brazilians to pee in the shower, on the theory that making your shower a little more golden can save each household over eleven hundred gallons of water each year in toilet flushes. I was going to make a big donation to the rain forest this year, but now I'm not sure—it turns out I've been doing my part for like thirty years.

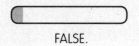

FALSE.

"Your Face Will Freeze Like That!" (Looks and Grooming)

"Yuck, get a Q-tip and clean out your ears!"

In 1923, a Jewish immigrant named Leo Gerstenzang watched his wife bathing their baby son, cleaning his ears with cotton balls she'd affixed to a toothpick. Gerstenzang worried that the boy might get hurt if the toothpick splintered or the cotton slipped off the tip, so he came up with a new solution: a small wooden stick with cotton already rolled securely around each end. He called his new invention "Baby Gays," later changed to "Q-tips" (the "Q" means quality!) for some reason, possibly because people weren't as cool with gay babies back in the 1920s as they are now.

Today, just as during that fateful 1923 bathtime, Q-tips are mostly used for "cleaning small orifices in and around the head," a Unilever VP admitted to *Time* in 1997. And yet every box of their fine cotton-tipped applicators reads, "WARNING: Do not insert into ear canal." That's exactly the same warning those alien earwig things had in *Star Trek II: The Wrath of Khan*! So basically Unilever sells over twenty-five billion Q-tips a year while winking and saying that they're for "household cleaning" or "makeup removal," fully knowing that we're making our ear-nose-and-throat doctors cringe by shoving them into our ears.

There are a few reasons to keep Q-tips (fine, Unilever lawyers, "or any other brand of cotton-tipped applicator") out of your ear canals. First, the swabs can actually pack down cerumen (the medical term for earwax) too close to the eardrum, rather than remove it. That's when you get earwax impaction and will need to see a doctor to avoid hearing loss and other serious damage. Earwax is also what keeps the delicate Georgia O'Keeffe painting of your ear innards lubricated and protected, and when you wipe it away too regularly, it can make the skin there dry, itchy, and even infected. The worst-case scenario is eardrum puncture, which can happen when someone is idly poking away at their ear with a swab and gets their elbow jostled somehow. Q-tip disappears, comes back out bloody. Eww. Back in the 1990s, when cotton-swab makers had to report cases like this to the FDA, there were twenty-odd "malfunctions" every year, but evidence from a 1993 court case in Missouri used hospital data to demonstrate that Q-tip users were actually going to emergency rooms at twenty-three times that rate.

Instead of probing around inside your ear with a swab or anything else, the American Academy of Otolaryngology recommends—well, doing nothing mostly. A little earwax is normal, and your daily jaw movements generally break it up and move it out of the ear naturally. If it builds up enough to cause health problems, you can try softening the wax with a few drops of mineral oil or glycerin, but if any manual cleaning or irrigation is needed, let a doctor take care of it. Whatever you do, don't fall for ear candling, the 1990s fad in which a candlelike cone of wax-soaked cloth is placed over the ear and lit on fire, magically "drawing out" a waxy residue. Spoilers: the waxy residue is *from the candle,* not your ear! Repeated studies have shown the candles will have no effect on your ear, except in cases where, say, the molten wax burns through your eardrum or the house catches fire and you die. (Both things have happened. A 1996 study published in *The Laryngoscope* found twenty-one serious ear-candling injuries.) Ear candling is to alternative medicine (nothing like actual medicine) what Limp Bizkit was to alternative rock (nothing like actual rock). But Q-tips are probably even worse for your ears, whether Mom recommended them or not.

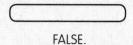

FALSE.

"Brush your hair one hundred times every night before bed!"

Do you take your hair-care advice from very old people? Or TV's Marcia Brady? If so, you may remember the old adage about one hundred strokes with a hairbrush being the magic number for beautiful, lustrous hair—not to mention another way to help women feel like they're perpetually falling short of some imaginary ideal!

The one-hundred-strokes rule might have made sense in a time when the nightly hair-brushing was *the* hair-care highlight of the day. In Grandma's day (see page 123) people washed their hair once every week or two and didn't spend the intervening time styling it with a vast array of treatments. In a world without modern shampoo, it was a good idea to brush a lot, to spread the oily mess at the scalp more evenly to the ends of the hair.

But today stylists and dermatologists generally believe people brush their hair too much, not too little. "Brush it out only to style it," says Philip Kingsley, founder of namesake trichological clinics in London and New York. ("Trichology" is the study of hair and the scalp.) "Brushing pulls hairs out of their follicles and possibly weakens individual strands." Marcia Marcia *Marcia*!

Most experts agree that fifteen to twenty strokes a day, using a gentle boar-bristle hairbrush or wide-toothed comb, are plenty to strengthen follicles and distribute natural oils—any more than that and you'll start breaking hairs and eroding their outer cuticle, which leads to tangles and split ends. As a middle-aged man, I'm not sure what any of those things are, but they sound *horrible*.

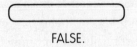

FALSE.

"If you pick your nose, it gets bigger!"

In anonymous polls, 91 percent of Americans admit to picking their noses. Forty-three percent say they pick in public, and 23 percent say they go at it for five to fifteen minutes at a stretch. We are a nation of nose pickers. And yet many people, apparently, were traumatized as children with the obvious falsehood that jabbing a finger up their nose could permanently alter its shape. It's the nasal equivalent of a priest's dire warnings about masturbation.

In fact, picking your nose may make your circle of friends smaller, but it won't make your nose or nostrils any bigger. Dr. Shervin Naveri is a Washington, DC–area facial plastic surgeon and rhinoplasty expert, so he knows what it takes to reshape the human nose. In most cases, he explained to me, bone and cartilage need to be surgically altered. Skin, however, can be stretched slightly over time, a property that surgeons call "creep." If a patient needs more skin to correct some defect, the tissues can be gradually expanded over time by placing balloon expanders under the skin. You see the same process at work in the earlobes or lips of certain East African tribal members, or that one record store clerk you hope won't be ringing you up. "However, nose picking is not a constant force," he said. "It is intermittent. Unless someone puts their thumb in their nose and leaves it there for several weeks, nose picking will *not* change the shape of the nostrils noticeably."

But parents are on safer ground warning their children that scraping around up there can lead to nosebleeds. Many doctors say that nose picking is, in fact, the number-one cause of nosebleeds in children, whereas in adults, dry air is usually to blame. Since I now know that adults pick their noses almost as much as kids, I can only assume that their technique and/or nail clipping has gotten better with age.

But even adults aren't totally immune from the dangers of rhinotillexomania, the clinical term for obsessive nose picking. In 2008, the British press reported the sad death of a Manchester man named Ian Bothwell, found by his landlord in such a bloody mess that everyone assumed he'd died by falling out of bed and banging his head. In fact, the coroner later discovered, he'd picked his nose so much that he bled to death from the resulting nosebleed. Moms and dads grossed out by nose picking offspring: this guy is your new cautionary tale/patron saint. You're welcome.

FALSE.

"Wear your retainer or your teeth will get crooked again!"

Nobody, except maybe lawyers, talks more about $200 retainers than orthodontists do. But the orthodontic kind of retainer isn't a fee; it's a plastic-and-wire dental device. If you never wore braces, you probably remember them as "those gross pink spitty things sitting on napkins on the corners of middle school cafeteria trays." I have a confession to make: when I got my teeth straightened, my orthodontist told me to wear my retainer day and night for a year or so, at which point I could graduate to nights only. Shamefully, I never wore it at all. Well, that's not true. I wore it for about a month, then dropped a schoolbook or something on it and cracked it in half. I was too embarrassed to get it replaced, so I never did.

But here's the punch line: my teeth still look great, the same as they did the day the braces came off. And I had my braces as an adult (well, "adult"—I was in college), which generally leads to more problems with stability. So what's the deal? Are retainers just a racket, either a way for dentists to gouge patients or a way to prop up the clear-pink-plastic industry now that kids don't play with Lite-Brite so much anymore?

Orthodontists insist that yes, retainers are crucial. "If you don't wear your retainer you will run the risk of your teeth shifting back to their original position," says dentist Marc Lazare in his *The Patient's Guide to Dentistry*. "The ligaments around the teeth have memory, and the more rotated your teeth were before, the more likely they will drift back without the proper retention." He goes on to say that patients should assume they'll be wearing their retainers *indefinitely* unless their orthodontist lets them off the hook. What a great way to feel sixteen forever.

Orthodontists speak from experience here; many know patients who had to get braces a second time because they didn't wear their retainer. My wife was an adult braces-wearer too (I think she got them around the time Tom Cruise did, just to be trendy), and she can feel the tightness when she goes a week or two without slipping in her retainer at night. But I'm living evidence that not every braces-wearer needs a retainer, and research shows that I'm not the first person ever to slack on wearing one. In 2011, orthodontists at Case Western discovered that there was almost no academic research on retainer use, so they undertook three studies. The first polled orthodontists and found that when they removed braces, most prescribed nine months of twenty-four-hour retainer use and part-time use thereafter. The second polled patients and found that I wasn't alone in my laziness. Only 60 percent wore retainers more than ten hours a day during the first three months. After a year and a half, 19 percent never wore them at all.

The third study—and this is where things get interesting—actually compared the smiles of retainer-wearers to those of the slackers: spacing, bite, tooth crowding, and so on. Nearly half the no-retainer patients showed no tooth movement at all, and some showed *positive* settling of the back teeth that retainers might have prevented. To be fair, though, others did get their teeth screwed up enough by the experiment that they had to go back to the orthodontist when it concluded.

The Case Western researchers say that more study is needed, but this much seems clear: some patients (like my wife) will need a retainer to keep their teeth looking great, while for other genetically superior ones (like me) it's a waste of time. Since there's no way to tell which group you're in, wearing a retainer is a smart choice—at least often enough to make sure your new teeth are stable. But I don't know if any amount of research will persuade parents to stop being such retainer

Nazis. Nobody wants to risk dropping another $5,000 on braces because Junior refused to wear a $200 retainer.

MOSTLY TRUE.

"If you keep wearing lip balm, your lips get 'addicted' to it!"

When I first heard this pearl of wisdom, it was specifically targeted at Carmex, the tiny lip balm jar with the yellow lid that seems to have fallen through a time warp every time you see it in a drugstore checkout lane. Carmex, obviously, hasn't changed much since it was first invented in 1937 in Wauwatosa, Wisconsin. The brain behind the balm was Alfred Woelbing, a bored department-store buyer who mixed up the first batch on a hot plate in his basement, and he and his family spent the next twenty years mixing Carmex in their kitchen and selling it out of the trunk of their car. To this day, the company never advertises, apart from the $10 a year it shelled out for Alfred's CARMEX vanity plate, prior to his 2001 death. Its customers inevitably discover its distinctive aroma and lip-soothing properties via word of mouth, and become fiercely loyal.

But are they loyal in the way that, say, a Boy Scout or golden retriever is loyal, or the way a heroin addict is loyal? For decades, Carmex (and to a lesser degree its competitors, from ChapStick to Blistex to Vaseline) has been dogged by accusations that its product is addictive. In its most sinister form, this bit of folklore claims that the Woelbing family has been stirring acid or ground fiberglass into those little jars for seventy-five years, in order to create a cycle of dependency in its users—er, customers. No evidence has ever been offered for any of these claims (the "acid" in Carmex is salicylic acid, a component of aspirin used in many skin products), but they seem to ring true for thousands of people. In 1995, a Bay Area corporate librarian named Kevin Crossman created a tongue-in-cheek twelve-step website called Lip Balm Anonymous to address his "problem" with ChapStick. More than fifteen years later, the site is still going strong, and millions of visitors, both in on the joke and not, have stopped by to seek help in their struggle with the cherry-scented monkey.

When journalists look into this phenomenon, they can usually find skin or beauty experts willing to point out that lip balms do contain ingredients that, with overuse, might irritate the skin in certain sensitive people—fragrances, for example, or the camphor or menthol that gives lip balms their cool tingle. But skin is finicky enough that lots of things *can* irritate it, including plain soap and water. The real problem with lip balm is that, like anything else, it can become a psychological dependency. The president of Blistex told *SmartMoney* in 2010 that when his company does focus groups on their heaviest users, they're inevitably fidgety types with other nervous habits: the pencil-biters, the nail-chewers. In other words, ChapStick and Carmex and all the rest don't cause chemical dependencies—they're just handy props for compulsives. If your lips are dry, give them a smear; otherwise, leave the tube in your pocket. It'll help you learn to stop worrying and love the balm.

MOSTLY FALSE.

"You're not fat. You're just big-boned!"

Skeletal weight, obviously, varies between people. If, heaven forbid, future archaeologists were someday to happen upon the ruins of an auditorium where the ESPY Awards had been taking place centuries before, they wouldn't have any trouble telling Shaquille O'Neal's skeleton apart from Kristi Yamaguchi's. When you leave height out of the equation, however, the differences between the "big-boned" and "small-boned" are surprisingly, well, slim.

The medical rule of thumb is that having an unusually large or small frame can make a 10 percent difference in what your healthy weight range should be. How to calculate whether your genetic heritage entitles you to (or saddles you with, according to your point of view) that extra 10 percent? Wrist size is usually the best indicator of how bulky or petite you'd be without all that annoying muscle, fat, and skin in the way. If you have a tape measure handy, there are actually detailed charts to show you what your wrist circumference might mean depending on your height. But if you're okay with a ballpark estimate, wrap the thumb and middle finger of one hand around your opposite wrist. If they touch, more or less, your frame size is average. If they overlap, you're an elfin little waif of a sprite and your skeleton is probably wearing a leotard when you see it in X-rays. If they don't meet, your bones are officially "husky" or "stocky" or whatever your mom's favorite euphemism was.

But, again, the telltale wrist only affects body weight by 10 percent or so. By contrast, the difference between a mean "normal weight" body mass index, or BMI, and a mean overweight one is well over 25 percent. Obese people can easily weigh twice their healthy weight. So if you're obsessing about five stubborn pounds, your "big bones" could explain them. But the vast majority of overweight kids need to blame their eating habits, not their skeletons.

In 2011, anthropologists at North Carolina State published new evidence linking weight and bone size. By measuring 121 different femurs (yes, this is what might happen when you donate your body to science) they learned that overweight people do indeed have wider bones, because of differences in the amount of weight their skeletons have to carry as well as the different walking motions they tend to use. In other words, being big-boned doesn't make you fat, but being fat might eventually make you big-boned.

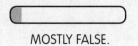

MOSTLY FALSE.

"Wash behind your ears! You could grow potatoes back there!"

Washing behind your ears is a good idea, of course, since that's an often-neglected part of the face that can get sweaty and oily. But the parental fixation on this particular zone has always seemed a little bit odd to me, bordering on the fetishistic. And let's squelch the potato thing in the bud right now: potato seeds need to be planted in three to four inches of soil. As long as the dirt behind your ears is less than three inches deep, you have nothing to worry about, tuber-wise.

One of Betty MacDonald's classic children's books about a neighborhood busybody named Mrs. Piggle-Wiggle features a horrifying chapter in which a hygienically challenged young girl named Patsy is persuaded to bathe more frequently by having radish seeds planted in the dirt caking her body. This is marginally more plausible, at least horticulturally, since radish seeds grow best when planted only a half inch deep. Still, their taproot is so large that Patsy's harvest wouldn't be a very successful one. I'm glad I could clear this up after all these years.

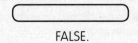

FALSE.

"It's All Fun and Games Until Someone Loses an Eye!" (Vision and Supervision)

"Don't cross your eyes or they'll stay like that!"

Permanently crossed eyes are a real medical condition, a type of strabismus called "esotropia." It's a lack of muscular coordination in the eyes—most often affecting just one eye, but in rare cases both—usually caused by a lesion in the cranial nerves. The opposite condition, exotropia, is a permanent wall-eyed stare, like the late Western character actor Jack Elam. (Remember Jack Elam? From *Rancho Notorious* and *Rio Lobo*? Oh, never mind.)

But strabismus is almost always a condition people are born with, arising from the way the optic nerves and muscles work. It can't be caused by sheer force of will. The ocular position we think of as "crossed eyes" isn't just an annoying kids' parlor trick—it's an exaggeration of the useful eye movement we all make to focus on close-up objects. Your eyes are no more likely to "stick" in that position than they are to freeze forever looking up, or to the left, or focused on something far away.

The only eye disorder that even slightly resembles the mythical "frozen crossed eyes" is accommodative esotropia, sometimes seen in farsighted people. These patients can only focus clearly on nearby objects by slightly crossing one of their eyes, and this reflex leads to a cross-eyed condition that can worsen over time if it's not corrected by glasses. But, I can't stress enough, this is caused by a congenital defect of the lens, not by a five-year-old amusing herself by making funny faces at her goldfish. In fact, a 1991 article on medical myth-debunking in *American Health* magazine pointed out that a child who's developed the muscular control to cross his eyes for long periods of time is just strengthening those muscles, meaning he's probably *less* likely than other kids to develop some cross-eyed complaint. No, this cockeyed myth is yet another case of parents saying, "That's dangerous!" when they really mean, "Why the hell are you doing that?"

FALSE.

"Don't wear someone else's glasses—it's bad for your eyes!"

I never needed glasses as a kid and felt keenly the pangs of eyewear envy toward my more scholarly looking peers. But every time I'd try on someone else's frames, I'd get the same reaction from shocked parents and schoolteachers: What are you doing? Wearing the wrong glasses will hurt your eyes! The cultural paranoia on this topic is so severe that the satirical newspaper *The Onion* used it as a gag on one of the covers to its faux Sunday supplement: a 2010 issue promised to reveal "The Life-Threatening DANGERS Of Trying On Someone Else's Glasses." Even some serious reference works have fallen for the hype. "Never wear glasses that are not your own," warns the 2004 *Encyclopedia of Family Health*.

Wearing the wrong glasses for extended periods of time can lead to eye fatigue and headaches, says the American Academy of Ophthalmology. The eyestrain is caused by the muscles in your eyes having to work in unexpected ways to focus; the headache is mostly due to your brain and inner ear being confused by the distorted visual stimuli they're trying to process. Your vision, of course, may be blurry as well.

But those are temporary conditions that will subside as soon as you remove the offending glasses. "Wearing a pair (of glasses) with the wrong lenses, or not wearing glasses at all, will not physically damage your eyes," says the ophthalmologists' organization. They do note that children under eight can develop amblyopia, or "lazy eye," if they wear the wrong prescription lenses *all the time,* but briefly joking around with a classmate's glasses isn't going to do the trick. I can speak from experience here: kids will get bored, or queasy, from Dad's glasses within minutes, long before they can screw up their delicate ocular muscles.

I don't recommend glasses swapping at school during your teenage years, however. It won't hurt your eyes, but there's going to be a *lot* of face grease on those frames.

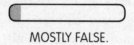

MOSTLY FALSE.

"Finish your carrots, they're good for your eyesight!"

The cliché about carrots improving your vision is often attributed to centuries-old herbal wisdom, sometimes as far back as the ancient Greeks. In fact, I haven't been able to find a single mention of this connection that predates the mid-1930s, when laboratories first started discovering that vitamin A deficiency led to night blindness—loss of vision in low-light conditions. These results certainly caught the public imagination. "The motorist with feeble eyesight is advised, before setting out for a night journey, to chew a carrot," wrote *The New York Times* in 1939. "The effect is, by all accounts, so salutary that some day there will doubtless be carrot filling stations beside all main roads. 'Standard Carrots—They Brighten the Way.' 'Gulfaco Carrots for Visibility.'"

Nineteenth-century herbal manuals recommend carrots for everything from epilepsy to chapped nipples to "restoring the wind of horses," but there's no mention of eyesight. Frustrated at not being able to trace the carrot myth back to its ancient, er, roots, I consulted William Woys Weaver, a food author and "vegetable historian" who runs the Keystone Center for the Study of Regional Foods and Food Tourism in Devon, Pennsylvania. According to Dr. Weaver, ancient and medieval botanists believed carrots repressed bile and moved urine (acted as a diuretic). "The only precaution," he told me, "was eating too many, since they affected the 'lower parts' and thus aroused 'ephebic pleasures'—sexual attraction to young men. Now, that would open some eyes, but I wouldn't call it a cure for glaucoma."

Yes, it's true: the ancients thought of carrots as a powerful aphrodisiac. This is a fairly common cultural belief all over the world regarding plants, like the carrot, that have a sufficiently phallic shape. Greeks even called the wild carrot "*philtron*," meaning "love potion." But Dr. Weaver agrees that improved vision was never cited as a side effect. "I have no idea when this carrots-for-the-eyes thing started—perhaps homeopathic health literature from Southern California, 1920s. It seems phony in any case."

This bit of folklore got its biggest boost during World War II, when Britain's Royal Air Force, no doubt aware of the recent discoveries about vitamin A and night vision, began to boast that its pilots' uncanny ability to shoot down German bombers over the English Channel could be chalked up to megadoses of carrots. Ace pilots like Group Captain John Cunningham became popular heroes and celebrities. To Cunningham's annoyance, he was nicknamed "Cat's Eyes" in the press, and his love of carrots became part of the myth that would follow him until his 2002 death.

In fact, the whole thing was a smoke screen. Nobody was eating carrots at British air bases; instead, the nation's military scientists had secretly invented airborne radar devices and installed them in fighter planes beginning in 1939. The carrot dodge was a way to keep the public—and the Germans—in the dark about this crucial technological advantage, one that probably saved thousands of lives during the Blitz.

The cover story was so effective that people still believe it today, seventy years later. It's true that carrots are an unusually rich source of vitamin A: just half a carrot with lunch will give you your entire recommended daily dose of beta-carotene. Eat more than three carrots a day, and your skin will gradually take on a yellowish-orange tinge. (Not a Willy Wonka trick! Actual scientific fact!) But vitamin A deficiency is only a problem in the developing world, where it affects almost fourteen million kids. It's almost unknown in North America. Not eating vitamin A *ever* will, indeed, keep your eyes from producing the retinal proteins called opsins that make vision possible, and you'll quickly go night-blind, followed eventually by blind-blind. But eating *extra* vitamin A isn't going to give your kids superhero vision.

In the elderly, it may be a different story, however. No link has ever been found between beta-carotene and cataract prevention, but a 2008 study by a UCLA ophthalmologist found that an extra serving or two of carrots a week lowered older women's risk of glaucoma by a whopping 69 percent. Still, eight-year-olds aren't huge glaucoma risks, so if you're using this as a way to get the kids to finish their veggies, it's a big lie. At that age, the only way you can improve kids' vision with carrots is to keep them from poking them in each other's eyes.

MOSTLY FALSE.

"Never sneeze with your eyes open—your eyeballs will pop out!"

Etiquette question: if you're with someone who sneezes, and their eye pops out of its socket and dangles on a thin gristle of optic nerve in front of their cheek, do you have to say "Gesundheit"? Or does "Dear *Lord*!" and a series of dry heaves suffice?

When we sneeze, the medulla oblongata at the base of the brain mediates a reflex that contracts lots of body muscles and sphincters. Scientists aren't sure if the eye-closing reflex is a side effect of that or if it's a useful adaptation of its own—perhaps to keep flying particles and microbes out of our eyes once we've sneezed them out? In any case, it's difficult, but not impossible, to sneeze with one's eyes open. A quick search of YouTube videos will turn up several people who have the knack. One of these superpowered mutants, a teenager named Jade, has been watched over 1.3 million times sneezing with her eyes wide open. And no, they don't fall out.

Surprisingly, however, there is a kernel of truth to this most outrageous of all playground rumors. Sneezing is a common trigger for an eye trauma called orbital emphysema, in which air from the sinuses floods into the eye socket, leading to puffiness and pain in the best-case scenario and loss of vision in the worst. The medical literature on orbital emphysema mentions a handful of cases dating back to 1845 in which the sneeze was so severe it caused "dislocation of the globe." (The "globe" here isn't the planet Earth—that would be one hell of a sneeze. "Globe" is another word for "eyeball.")

Having an eye pop out of its socket is a fairly uncommon medical condition, but it does happen. Doctors call it "spontaneous globe luxation," and a 2002 paper collected reports of twenty-six different cases. In 79 percent of the cases, fiddling with the eyelids was enough to cause the eye to pop out, but in other cases, sneezing, nose blowing, crying, coughing, or just bending over did the trick. One such sneezer was Mary Hanrehan, an Indianapolis woman who sneezed an eye out on a streetcar, according to an April 1882 *Indianapolis Times* article. A 1951 news report says the same thing happened to George Miller, a Saint Louis attorney casually watching TV at home. Mr. Miller popped the eye back in and never lost any vision, though Ms. Hanrehan was not so lucky.

"Acute globe subluxation, when it occurs, is quite alarming for the patient as well as hospital staff," says one medical text, with remarkable understatement, "and requires urgent medical attention to avoid potentially devastating complications." In the most severe cases, the eyeball comes out far enough that the eyelid can actually shut behind it. (Eww. But useful for seeing behind you while parallel parking.) The treatment is simple: doctors numb the area with painkillers, then manually shove the eye back in the socket, pushing on the white part of the eye and/or shoehorning it into place with a bent paper clip. Sure, this sounds horrible, but it's not like you to have to watch every second of it! Oh, wait. Yes, you do.

But there's no evidence that any of these injuries were caused by an eyes-open sneeze. The eyeball, after all, is held in place by six sturdy muscles, *not* by the eyelids, which aren't strong enough. If you're unlucky enough to have an eyeball-detonating sneeze percolating in your sinuses right now, it won't matter what you do with your eyes—that eyeball is coming out anyway. Either way, God bless you.

MOSTLY FALSE.

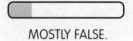

"It's too dark to read in here, you'll hurt your eyes!"

Young Abe Lincoln famously read late into the night by candlelight, but today's kids don't get the same presidential privileges. Moms and dads *love* to walk around turning on lights when kids are reading or watching TV. It's a perk of the job. As a bonus, they also get to complain later about all the lights being left on all the time. "Do you kids think electricity is free around here?"

This timeless parental nag transcends international boundaries. A 2006 study from Pakistan found that 56 percent of schoolteachers scolded kids for reading in dim light, while only 9 percent of the kids thought it was bad for their eyes. In this case, the kids are all right: there's no evidence linking reading in the dark to eye problems. "Using your eyes in dim light does not damage them," says the American Academy of

Ophthalmology. "However, good lighting does make reading easier and prevent eye fatigue."

The human eye evolved during our hunter-gatherer period to do lots of things well, but moving from left to right over extremely close objects at high speed for hours on end wasn't one of them. Reading too much can tire your eyes, no matter how many lights are on. When light is dim, it does take more effort for the eye to focus on the page, and you might get dry or achy eyes or blurred vision sooner. But a few minutes' eye rest will clear it right up.

Some researchers have wondered if the twenty-first-century rigors we put our eyes through (hours of reading, computer monitors, etc.) might have long-term effects we haven't studied well enough yet. An oft-cited study here is one published in 1969 that looked at the eyes of twelve hundred Inuits in Barrow, Alaska, the northernmost city in the United States. Myopia, or nearsightedness, was unknown in their community before they were introduced to modern culture during World War II. By the 1960s, the older generation still had a zero-percent incidence of myopia, but an astounding 88 percent of the children under twenty were nearsighted.

There's still no scientific consensus on the linkage between reading or TV watching and myopia. But even if our eye-straining modern lives make our kids more prone to vision problems—and I'll stress again that most eye doctors still think that's not true—it doesn't mean that reading in low light is one of these factors. As the American Academy of Ophthalmology points out, "For centuries, all nighttime reading and sewing was done by candlelight or with gas or kerosene lamps." In other words, we're living in an unprecedented golden age of well-lit reading, so if nearsightedness is getting worse, our proximity to the living room table lamp probably isn't to blame. Abe Lincoln, after all, didn't need reading glasses until he was almost fifty.

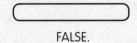

FALSE.

My mom always plopped us back on the couch if we were watching cartoons on the carpet in front of the television. The couch was safe and healthy; the carpet was dangerous. I always thought this was yet another of mom's never-ending warnings about things that caused eyestrain (like reading in dim light, above). It never occurred to me that she might have been worried about actual rays coming out of the screen and injuring us. Bizarrely, in the late 1960s, that's exactly what was happening in living rooms all across America.

In 1967, General Electric announced that 110,000 of its larger color televisions were emitting unsafe levels of X-rays, as high as 100,000 times the recommended standard, due to faulty voltage regulators. The U.S. surgeon general, William Stewart, recommended staying away from the sides and rear of the sets and sitting at least six feet away from the screen. If that's the generation of tube watching that produced your parents, their caution may be understandable—but it's also forty-five years out of date, since the faulty sets were quickly recalled.

"Contrary to popular myth, sitting too close to a TV will not damage your eyes, but it may cause eyestrain," says Dr. Lee Duffner of the American Academy of Ophthalmology. "Children can focus at close distance without eyestrain better than adults. Therefore, children often develop the habit of holding reading materials close to their eyes or sitting right in front of the TV." This kind of thing can fatigue the eyes, leading to headache and blurred vision, but it doesn't cause any lasting damage. A short break will usually take care of the problem. For today's screen-obsessed kids, doctors recommend something called the "20–20–20 rule": every twenty minutes, take a twenty-second break from the hypnotic glowing screen to look at something twenty feet away.

As we saw in the previous entry, there's no clear evidence linking eyestrain to myopia, or nearsightedness—in fact, most cases of myopia are 100 percent genetic. But myopia might be a cause, not a result, of sitting too close to the TV. A child who prefers to be mere inches away from *SpongeBob* might need an eye exam to see if she's nearsighted. Of course, too much TV can have other, non-ophthalmological side effects, like obesity, imitative behavior, and unusually expert familiarity with the *iCarly* supporting cast. But those mostly depend on your distance from reality, not from the TV screen.

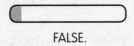

FALSE.

"Don't look in the microwave while it's running!"

Ninety percent of American households now have a microwave oven, so many of you don't even remember a time when there *was* no three-minute popcorn option in the kitchen. But older readers will recall the arrival of the big, newfangled monstrosity that Grandma pursed her lips at, wondering what this Atomic Age menace (invented by the Nazis; that's what Edith at church told me) was doing to our insides. I came of age in the 1970s, and my parents were adamant that my siblings and I *never* look at the hypnotically spinning platter of the microwave while it was running. Of course, I was fascinated. What was going on there that was so forbidden?

Go look closely at your microwave door. Bring this book with you if you like. What appears from a distance to be some kind of tinted glass is, in fact, a fine metal mesh, full of little round holes that let you see if the cheese in your burrito is oozing out yet. The metal mesh, along with the metal lining the other surfaces of the oven, is crucial to microwave safety, because it makes the oven interior, in effect, into a Faraday cage, a scientific device used to block electric fields. Notice that the holes in the mesh are only a millimeter or two in diameter.

The radiation that cooks your food travels at a much longer wavelength, twelve centimeters or so. (Despite their name, microwaves are among the longest waves in the electromagnetic spectrum. They're only "micro" in comparison to radio waves.) This means visible light can get through the mesh easily, but microwaves have a much harder time.

The U.S. safety standard for microwave oven emissions is minuscule—five milliwatts of radiation per square centimeter of surface area from a distance of five centimeters away from the oven—and today's microwave ovens come out of the box ten times safer. "There is little cause for concern about excess microwaves leaking from ovens," says the Food and Drug Administration. "In FDA's experience, most ovens tested show little or no detectable microwave leakage." A microwave door that gets gunky over time or gets slammed a lot might conceivably lose some of its shielding mojo. If you have reason to think your microwave door seals are faulty for some reason, don't check it out with those leakage sensors you can buy at a hardware store, which aren't very accurate. Instead, get your oven tested by a state or government health agency.

You can find plenty of antimicrowave literature from the same electromagnetic-field-paranoia industry that fuels worries about cell phones or power lines causing cancer, despite all available evidence to the contrary. But the FDA says, "There are no established adverse health effects, including cancer, from using or standing in front of a standard microwave oven." Microwaves have been in kitchens for forty years with no demonstrated health risks and without a single radiation-related injury being reported, but the FDA still hedges its bets against the once-harmless ovens suddenly being revealed as a terrible menace, as has recently happened with the sun, and trans fats, and Mexican immigrants. "As an added safety precaution," read its guidelines, "don't stand directly against an oven (and don't allow children to do this) for long periods of time while it is operating."

So there you have it: the only concerns are of proximity, in case scientists of the far-flung future find some link between leaky microwaves and leukemia or sterility or something. There's no reason to think the eyes can be affected. Leaning against the microwave "for long periods of time" is out, if you want to be extra-cautious, but peering in to get the latest info on your Hot Pocket is just fine. Let me know what you see in there—I'm still too inhibited by my childhood to bring myself to look.

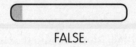

FALSE.

"Don't look at the sun, you'll go blind!"

Of all the things parents warn their kids not to stare at (the microwave, the TV, the fat guy at the supermarket), we've finally hit upon one that is medically justified: the sun. It's true: Mr. Sun is really, really bright, even from ninety-three million miles away. By my math, the sun looks about one thousand times more luminous to human eyes than a one-hundred-watt lightbulb across the room, which explains why childhood birthday photos taken indoors without a flash look so dungeonlike.

It's often said that the astronomer Galileo went blind in his old age as a result of a lifetime of looking at the sun. In fact, Galileo was well aware of the risks, and his solar observations were done by projecting the sun's image onto a screen behind his telescope, the same way amateur astronomers are told to look at eclipses today. He did go blind in his final years, but that was a result of cataracts and glaucoma. I don't know of any verified medical cases of someone going totally blind from the sun, because human reflexes (pupil contraction, eventually averting the eyes) typically kick in to the save the stupid. A popular 1960s urban legend warned straight-facedly of a group of acid-dropping hippies in Santa Barbara who suffered a phenomenally "bad trip," as the young people would say, when LSD made them stare at the sun for minutes on end. Those news reports, however, turned out to be a hoax.

But it is possible to damage your vision by looking too long at the sun, a condition ophthalmologists call "solar retinopathy." Doctors have seen a rash of such cases many times in the past: after solar eclipses, for example, or in 2009 when a group of Catholic pilgrims in Ireland stared at the sun in hopes of seeing a vision of the Virgin Mary. During the Vietnam era, sun-staring to cause partial blindness was even used to avoid the draft. My parents used to warn that eye damage was possible even when the sun didn't "feel" dangerously bright, because its ultraviolet rays could still be harmful, even at sunrise or sunset. In fact, that's a fairly minor concern. Ultraviolet rays can cause a kind of corneal inflammation called keratitis that leads to snow blindness or the eye damage sometimes seen in arc-welders, and eye doctors recommend a lifetime of UV-absorbing eyewear on bright days to prevent cumulative damage to the cornea and retina. But according to NASA's eye safety guidelines, the real danger in solar observation is visible light.

Most of the damage that's done is photochemical: the rod and cone cells of the retina become less sensitive under a barrage of intense light, and given enough exposure, the effect can be permanent. Keep looking long enough or often enough, though, and the combination of visible and infrared light will begin to literally cook the retina thermally. Imagine a magnifying glass focusing sunlight on a sizzling grape, and you'll get the idea. Because there are no pain receptors in the retina, you won't even be aware of the damage until several hours later, when the vision problems kick in. In most cases, the damage is reversible, but it might persist for up to a year.

Kids' eyes are more sensitive to retinopathy than adults' are, but it still takes longer than a quick glance to do even temporary damage—doctors estimate thirty seconds or so. So there's no need to fly off the handle every time kids look at the sun. It doesn't mean they'll grow up to be "sun-gazers," faddists who spend minutes a day pondering the sun for iffy health or spiritual reasons. Many sun-gazers claim that the practice is an important part of their "breathatarianism"— that is, that looking at the sun provides them with so many nutrients that they don't even need to eat anymore. If you start to notice a lot of really skinny blind people, you'll know it's catching on.

MOSTLY TRUE.

"You'll shoot your eye out!"

The name of the first turn-of-the-twentieth-century parent to worry that their little boy would "shoot his eye out" with a BB gun is lost in the mists of time and alcohol. But humorist and radio raconteur Jean Shepherd immortalized the warning in his nostalgic 1964 *Playboy* short story "Duel in the Snow, or Red Ryder Nails the Cleveland Street Kid," and it unexpectedly became an archetypal mass-culture catchphrase when a low-budget 1983 movie adaptation of Shepherd's short fiction, *A Christmas Story*, became a holiday perennial.

The United States is one of the only nations in the world that doesn't regulate the sale of air guns, though many municipalities have stricter laws. As a result, these weapons, considered firearms in much of the world, are still popular items on toy store shelves and in kids' letters to Santa in this country. Never mind that air guns can propel ammo at speeds up to 1,200 feet per second, substantially overlapping the muzzle velocities of handgun cartridges. Even the "Official Red Ryder Carbine-Action 200 Shot Range Model Air Rifle," still as popular with kids as it was in Jean Shepherd's day, shoots BBs at 350 feet per second—the length of a football field; not too shabby. And yet, more than three million nonpowder guns are sold yearly, most to young people.

Obviously, not every new owner of a Daisy Red Ryder air rifle catches a ricochet in the eye on Christmas morning, like Ralphie does in *A Christmas Story*. But, according to numbers from the National Electronic Injury Surveillance System, air guns are still the cause of more injuries to children than any other item you'd find under a Christmas tree, with the exception of bikes and skating equipment. According to a 2004 review by the American Academy of Pediatrics, nonpowder guns killed thirty-nine Americans over the previous decade, almost all of them children, and cause about twenty-two thousand injuries a year. In 2010, almost a third of the reported accidents were, indeed, to the eye, just like Mom warned.

The pediatricians found that air gun injuries, for the most part, need to be treated just like low-velocity firearms injuries, and that their "seriousness . . . is frequently underestimated," not just because of the popular perception of the guns as toys, but also because of the small, easy-to-miss projectiles and entry wounds involved. As a result, they say, these injuries tend to be rare but catastrophic.

It's easy to find YouTube videos of gun nuts' children as young as four or five enjoying their first assault rifle, but parents who *aren't* cousins as well as spouses may want to pay closer attention to the age recommendations on the box. Daisy warns that its Red Ryder rifle isn't safe for children under ten, period. Other guns with higher muzzle velocities shouldn't be used by anyone under sixteen.

I'm not saying that BB guns aren't fun or that they can't be used safely. I dare you to name me a better dad in the history of great dads than Atticus Finch, and he famously told his son that air guns were fine, as long as he remembered it was a sin "to kill a mockingbird." Daisy and the other air rifle manufacturers are scrupulous nowadays about reminding parents that their products aren't toys and that buyers need to follow strict rules like "never point the muzzle at another person" and "wear eye protection," which will give them practice handling real guns safely later on, if that's what they're into. But supervision and structure are going to be required if you want your little Ralph or Randy to reach adulthood with both eyes intact. Otherwise, take your lead from *A Christmas Story* and stick to a nice football or pink bunny pajamas. Or a toy zeppelin.

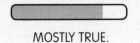

MOSTLY TRUE.

"Don't Let the Bedbugs Bite!"
(The Science of Sleep)

"Don't eat that right before bed, you'll have bad dreams!"

In Dickens's *A Christmas Carol,* the miserly Scrooge doesn't believe, at first, that his late partner Jacob Marley has come back from the grave to visit him. "You may be an undigested bit of beef, a blot of mustard, a crumb of cheese, a fragment of an underdone potato!" he rails. This belief, that indigestion can lead to nightmares, has been a medical assumption going as far back as the Roman physician Galen. At the turn of the twentieth century, one of the most popular newspaper cartoons in America was *Dream of the Rarebit Fiend,* by Winsor McCay, the cartoonist who would go on to create the classic *Little Nemo in Slumberland.* In every *Rarebit Fiend* strip, the protagonist would find himself engulfed in some frightening or surreal experience—only to wake up and blame the "rarebit" (melted cheese on toast) that he'd eaten before bed. Yes, this was the state of popular entertainment in 1904: you could draw a successful comic strip about the health consequences of eating grilled cheese sandwiches.

For much of the next century, sleep researchers continued to assume that nightmares were mostly a result of tummy troubles. The only argument was over whether indigestion affected dreams by cramping the circulation or if it affected the nervous system directly. I myself have noticed unusually vivid dreams after eating a big holiday meal or spicy lamb vindaloo. But, anecdotes like mine aside, it turns out there's no good scientific evidence of food causing nightmares.

Dr. Ernest Hartmann, a professor of psychiatry at Tufts University, is one of the world's foremost experts on sleep and dreams, with over fifty years' work in the field. For his 1984 book *The Nightmare,* he tested out what he calls the "pepperoni pizza" hypothesis with one hundred frequent nightmare sufferers. Only one reported a correlation between diet and nightmares. Dr. Hartmann attributes most nightmares to psychological stress, but notes that, if a big evening meal leads to fitful sleep, it's possible that sleepers, waking more often, would be more likely to *remember* their dreams. The only subsequent study on this phenomenon was reported by a 1992 paper from the University of Tasmania: "Spicy meal disturbs sleep: an effect of thermoregulation?" These researchers found that when they fed mustard and Tabasco sauce to subjects, they did indeed take longer to fall asleep and they got less of the slow-wave sleep that refreshes the brain. However, they reported no changes to the subjects' REM sleep, when dreams occur, so as I see it, the jury is still out.

The only other research I could find on this topic was a 2005 British study that fed cheese to two hundred subjects before bedtime to see if the "Rarebit Fiend" superstition about cheese causing nightmares is true. No, say the researchers. None of the patients reported nightmares, and 72 percent slept well every night of the survey. Reading on, I see that subjects who ate Stilton cheese reported the most unusual dreams, including one about a sad vegetarian crocodile. Eating cheddar led to dreams about celebrities, while red Leicester made them dream about being back in school. Wait, what the?—aha. I see now. This "study" was sponsored by the British Cheese Board as a PR stunt and the press release went out under the heading "Sweet dreams are made of cheese." Okay, never mind then.

That said, it doesn't seem *impossible* to me that there's some connection between diet and nightmares, even if it hasn't yet been proven. We know certain foods disrupt sleep. We know certain pharmaceutical drugs and fever-causing illnesses can lead to nightmares. Food certainly contains compounds with medicinal properties and can affect body temperature as well, so you never know. Dr. Hartmann may not be convinced, but he was studying people with frequent nightmares— it stands to reason that, for the rest of us, *our* occasional nightmares might sometimes be brought on by Taco Bell, even if theirs have clearer psychological roots. If you ask me, more research is urgently needed here. All it's going to take is one sleep lab well stocked with Thai food, and we could blow the lid off this thing.

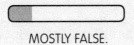

MOSTLY FALSE.

"You're yawning, must be bedtime!"

"If you cough, sneeze, sigh or yawn," wrote future president George Washington, copying out etiquette rules as a schoolboy, "do it not loud but privately, and speak not in your yawning, but put your handkerchief or hand before your face and turn aside." The association of yawning with fatigue or boredom has long made it more taboo than other ugly facial contortions. Laughing loudly or singing may show someone your spitty tongue and uvula, but yawning is even worse. Yawning says, "Look at my spitty tongue and uvula *because your company is tedious!*"

Or does it? Parents have long used yawning as an excuse to convince kids they need an early bedtime, but the reflex is still poorly understood. "We can put a man on the moon, but we do not understand what the function of yawning is," says yawning researcher Gary Hack.

The mechanism of yawning was long explained as a function of low blood oxygen. Tired people take shallower breaths, and this could explain why we yawn more when we're fatigued. It's true that scientists have been able to induce yawning in lab rats by lowering oxygen levels in a part of their hypothalamus called the paraventricular nucleus, which appears to be the "yawning center" of the brain. But people have been shooting holes in the oxygen theory for years. Fetuses yawn in utero, for example, even though that obviously won't put more oxygen in their lungs. And a 1987 experiment by Dr. Robert Provine, perhaps the world's greatest expert on yawning, showed that when subjects breathed air with higher carbon dioxide levels, their yawning didn't increase at all.

Then there's the whole matter of contagious yawning. If yawning is just a way to oxygenate tired lungs, then why do people yawn within five minutes, 55 percent of the time, when they see someone else yawn? Why would this reflex be more powerful in very empathic people and less prominent in people with autism-spectrum disorders? Why would it even be contagious across species borders? (Yes, you can make your dog yawn, but don't get too cocky. A chimp could make you yawn as well, if he really wanted to.) Obviously yawning isn't just a way to take a deeper breath—it's also a way for organisms to communicate information about their well-being to the rest of their population.

Much of the latest research centers on yawning as a means of heat exchange. Dr. Andrew Gallup of New York's Binghamton University has collected a series of interesting results demonstrating that yawning is actually the way an overheated brain cools off. He's been able to measure a temperature drop in the brains of yawning lab rats and induce yawning in parakeets by warming their surroundings. In 2011, he demonstrated seasonal variation in contagious human yawning for the first time: subjects yawned twice as much during the Arizona winter as they did in summer, when the ambient air is so hot it wouldn't actually cool the brain.

A yawning eight-year-old, then, could have "caught" the yawn from elsewhere (contagious yawning begins at age four), or she could just be a little warm, but Dr. Gallup says the kid is probably warm *because* she's tired. "Sleep and body temperature vary inversely," he told a newspaper reporter, "so extended sleep deprivation significantly increases brain and body temperature." A cool yawn wakes us up the same way a cold shower does. If he's right, we evolved yawning as a way to stimulate alertness and arousal, and communicate that fact to the rest of the pack. So a yawn doesn't mean that we're bored—in fact, Gallup calls it "a mechanism that maintains attention, and therefore should be looked at as a compliment!" Try that one out on your boss and let me know how it goes over.

MOSTLY TRUE.

"Early to bed, early to rise!"

In 1735, Benjamin Franklin told the readers of his *Poor Richard's Almanack,* "Early to bed and early to rise makes a man healthy, wealthy, and wise," but he didn't invent the rhyme. It was around at least a hundred years before, to judge by seventeenth-century proverb collections by English authors like John Clarke and James Howell, from whom Franklin borrowed liberally. The great bifocal-inventor himself seems to have been a poor student of his own advice, telling the *Journal de Paris* in 1784 that he'd been surprised recently to be awoken at dawn, since he usually had "never seen any signs of sunshine before noon."

We know now that, while the circadian rhythms of our bodies do keep all of us strictly regulated to a twenty-four-hour cycle, there are widely varying individual sleep profiles, or "chronotypes," within that cycle. Research on families suggests that our chronotype is largely a genetic predilection. It's been shown that kids' bodies can adjust to bedtime being moved back or forth an hour or so, but in general, there's no way to turn an early bird (sleep researchers call them "larks") into a night owl (sleep researchers call them, duh, "owls") or vice versa. As you get older, your chronotype may gradually change— teenagers are usually owls, fiftysomethings are larks—but it's not a change that can be forced by light exposure, melatonin, or hectoring parents.

It's easy to find sleep studies trumpeting the value of an early bedtime for kids, but in most cases, the better health or school performance or whatever was a result of getting *more sleep,* not the specific hours at which that sleep occurred. A 1998 study in the *British Medical Journal* specifically targeted Franklin's advice by assembling groups of over three hundred larks and owls and comparing their lifespan (healthy), mean income (wealthy), and cognitive function (wise). Surprisingly, the only difference was in income, where the owls had a slight advantage over the morning people. Both groups lived longer, on average, than people who *didn't* stay up late or rise early, but that's because the study focused on senior citizens, a group whose oversleepers tend to die sooner. But a 2006 Canadian study on a wider set of age groups found essentially the same thing: no big differences in health, wealth, or wisdom as a result of sleep schedule.

A dissenting result has come from an Australian university, which found, in 2011, that early-bird kids and teens were more active and skinnier than their night-owl classmates. The sleeper-inners, who went to bed almost an hour and a half later than the early risers, were 1.5 times more likely to be obese and almost three times as likely to spend too much time with TV and video games. But even if this finding is borne out by more research, it may be a moot point, if there's no healthy way to turn night people into morning people.

As a night owl myself, I can tell you firsthand the struggles my people face in a world where school buses and morning work meetings often come far, far too early. Putting your kids to bed early may or may not coincide with their personal "chronotypes," but I'll grant you this: it may be the only way to get them the sleep they need before the morning school bell rings. (It also may prolong their lives by giving parents a few blessed kid-free hours every evening.) But I suspect the "early to bed, early to rise" advice maintains its currency for puritanical reasons, not practical ones. Going to bed early and getting up early are both things that aren't any fun. Therefore, according to a certain monastic and/or masochistic outlook, they must be good. By the same thinking, it must be healthy to sleep on a mayonnaise-covered mattress or use Hootie and the Blowfish as your alarm clock ring, because those things are unpleasant as well. But just being unpleasant doesn't automatically make something good for you.

I prefer the advice of James Thurber, who wrote a 1940 fable for *The New Yorker* called "The Shrike and the Chipmunks." It ends with the lazy-but-lovable chipmunk protagonist being killed by a bird because his early-rising wife insists on a brisk morning walk. The moral of Thurber's story? "Early to rise and early to bed makes a man healthy and wealthy and dead."

MOSTLY FALSE.

"Never wake a sleepwalker!"

This is good advice, but not for the reason that you think. Sleepwalking, or somnambulism, is surprisingly common, especially in children, with 30 percent of kids experiencing episodes from time to time. For centuries, we've been warned that waking a sleepwalker could lead to a heart attack, brain damage, or worse. In 1841, for example, a London surgeon named Walter Cooper Dendy solemnly related the case of "a young lady who was walking in a garden in her sleep; she was awoke, and almost instantly died."

I have no explanation for Dr. Dendy's secondhand report, because there's never been a verified case of spontaneous sleepwalker death in the medical literature. In reality, sleepwalkers, when suddenly awoken, are likely to be disoriented and even distressed by their unfamiliar surroundings, but that's as serious as it gets. To avoid a possible sock in the jaw, doctors recommend gently leading the sleepwalker back to bed rather than waking him or her. Waking a sleepwalker, in other words, is only dangerous for the waker, not for the sleeper.

In fact, the only serious injuries reported to sleepwalkers are in those cases where *nobody* woke them up. In 2007, a sleepwalking teen in Demmin, Germany, wandered out of a fourth-floor apartment window. He fell thirty feet to the ground, breaking an arm and a leg—and went on peacefully sleeping.

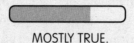

MOSTLY TRUE.

"This Room Is a Pigsty!" (Kids and Other Animals)

"Don't touch its wings, or the butterfly will die!"

If you've ever touched a butterfly, you probably noticed that its wings left a fine powder on your fingertips. Well-meaning parents or teachers may have scolded you for your crimes against class Insecta, saying that removing any of the powder from its wings will doom a butterfly to certain death. Some might even have added the old wives' tale that the dust will cause blindness if it gets in your eyes.

Neither claim is true, though. The powder you see on your fingers after touching a butterfly is made up of the tiny scales that cling to its wings. (Butterflies and moths belong to order Lepidoptera, from the Latin for "scaly wings.") Each butterfly wing is covered with over one hundred million of these tiny scales, but they aren't used in flight. Instead, they provide the colorful patterns that the butterfly may use for camouflage, mating, or defense against predators. Most of the brightest colors you see on butterfly wings are the result of microscopic ridges on the scales, not any pigment. In other words, the scales themselves aren't colored pink or blue or green—it just *looks* like they are. (Apparently, this involves photonic crystallite nanostructures. Just take my word for it.)

The butterfly's scales aren't attached all that firmly to the wing—any contact during the course of its day, even by the softest of bunnies or dewiest of dewdrops, will rub off a few. But since the butterfly carries over a hundred million spares, it generally survives such encounters unscathed. Scientists who mark butterflies for tracking purposes will routinely scrape away enough scales to tag the clear membrane beneath, and the butterfly flies away like nothing ever happened.

Butterfly wings are fragile, of course, and clumsy little fingers might do worse than dislodge scales when they go grabbing—they could tear a wing or pull off a leg, which *could* be fatal. So teach kids to be careful with butterflies. The safest way to hold one is to wait until its wings are all together in a vertical position, and then hold all four wings lightly between your index and middle fingers. Even if a few scales are left behind, the butterfly can still go on to live a long and happy life. Well, a month or two. That's long by butterfly standards.

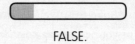

FALSE.

"Don't pick up that dirty feather!"

Kids are endlessly fascinated by feathers they find on the sidewalk or playground. Parents, on the other hand, get totally skeeved out by them. If my mom were compiling a list of the scariest screen villains of all time, I think she'd ignore Darth Vader or Freddy Krueger in favor of "that feather from the beginning of *Forrest Gump*."

But the Cornell Lab of Ornithology disagrees. "It is safe to pick up feathers where there have been no outbreaks of avian flu from the highly pathogenic H5N1 virus," says its website. In 2006, four people in Azerbaijan died from bird flu after defeathering swans, but all of North America remains untouched by bird flu. Dr. Mindy LaBranche, project coordinator at the lab, told *The New York Times* that most bird lice and mites don't even spread among bird species well, much less to humans. And a feather on the ground has probably been off the bird long enough to be fairly parasite-free. Some diseases, like histoplasmosis, are transmitted by fungi found in bird feces, but a good hand-washing should take care of the risk. Bird feathers are no grosser than any of the hundreds of other things your kids could get their hands on while playing outside, and probably safer than some.

But if I can't talk you out of your feather-phobia, you can always threaten your kids with the full weight of the federal government. The 1918 Migratory Bird Treaty Act, written at a time when bird feathers were much in demand as hat ornaments and writing implements, is still U.S. law, so it's still a federal crime to possess almost any bird, feather, nest, or egg. That's right: a feather found on the ground is just as illegal as one plucked off the tail of a majestic bald eagle in flight. (The law had to be written this way, or it would have been unenforceable.) A few nonnative species like pigeons, sparrows, and starlings are specifically excepted by the law, but almost every other bird in your backyard is protected.

The law is occasionally still trotted out when people get caught making and selling handicrafts from large quantities of bird feathers. A SWAT team is, of course, unlikely to come crashing into your five-year-old's bedroom tonight to seize the crow feather she found at the park. But if you want them to leave feathers alone, your kids don't have to know that!

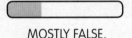

MOSTLY FALSE.

"Don't feed the dog chocolate!"

I've pooh-poohed lots of other poisoning risks in this book, from poinsettias to toothpaste, but this one is actually legit: dogs shouldn't have chocolate. In other words, man's best friend and woman's best friend don't mix.

The culprit here is theobromine, the same alkaloid that gives humans that great chocolate buzz but is much harder for other animals to metabolize. A dog can take seventeen hours to metabolize half of a dose of theobromine, which is why chocolate is the single most common toxin reported to vets and pet poison lines. And we're not just talking an upset tummy here: the toxic dose depends on the size of the dog and the purity of the chocolate involved, but a few ounces of baking chocolate can be all it takes to kill a medium-sized dog. Cats are even more susceptible, but in practice, this is less of an issue, because all good-hearted people like cats less than dogs. No! Just kidding. It comes up less because a cat's tongue has no taste receptors for sweetness, so most will turn up their noses at a candy bar.

This doesn't mean you have to panic every time your dog finds an M&M under the armchair, but Wonka-sized chocolate quantities need to be kept out of their reach, and kids should know which treats aren't dog-safe. Chocolate isn't the only forbidden substance: sugarless candy and gum often contain the artificial sweetener xylitol, which is known to cause low blood sugar and even liver failure in dogs, and grapes and raisins have recently been linked to dog deaths as well. No one is quite sure why, though a still-unidentified fungus is presumed to be responsible. And macadamia nuts can make a dog stagger around as if drunk for a day or two. So there you have it, dog lovers: you own a pet that will happily drink out of the toilet and eat its own poop but can be laid low by a bowl of chocolate/macadamia/raisin/Tic Tac trail mix. There's no accounting for taste.

TRUE.

"Don't give those bones to the dog!"

Despite what you have seen in every cartoon in the history of cartoons, dogs and bones are a bad match. I know this seems tragically wrong, as if we'd recently discovered that squirrels shouldn't eat acorns, or bears shouldn't eat honey, or Jamie Lee Curtis shouldn't eat that yogurt that makes you poop better. But it's true: the old-timey vet warnings about chicken bones have now been replaced by warnings against *any* type of bone at all, even pork or beef. Among the ten dire-sounding bone complications that the Food and Drug Administration lists in its antibone literature are broken teeth, blocked windpipes and intestines, rectal bleeding, and peritonitis. Mickey Mouse's dog, Pluto, always looked so happy when he had a big juicy bone in his doggy dish, but I guess Walt Disney never showed us the rectal bleeding that ensued after the cartoon ended.

Some pet owners continue to give their dogs uncooked bones with a clear conscience. This practice is defended especially vigorously by various kinds of raw food advocates who insist on imposing their current fad diet du jour onto their pets as well. It's true that bones do get more brittle when cooked, and are therefore less prone to dangerous splintering when they're raw. It's also true that dogs and their relatives undeniably chew on raw bones in the wild, and presumably many survive the ordeal—and with better teeth to boot, since bones keep dogs' teeth clean. But there are other ways to clean your canines' canines, and many vets and pet owners will find that the risks of giving bones to dogs outweigh the benefits. At a minimum, limit your dog to raw beef bones that are too big to swallow, and keep a close eye on them for digestive trouble afterward. You can always switch to chew toys or rawhide strips if bones continue to give you gnawing doubts.

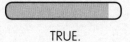

TRUE.

"If you touch that baby bird, its mommy will abandon it!"

Children have long been cautioned not to pick up a baby bird found struggling on the ground. According to folk wisdom, human contact can be fatal for young animals. If a baby bird has a whiff of human scent on it, the story goes, its mother will reject it from the nest, sort of like the way a human mother might suspiciously sniff her young for beer or pot.

The good news for adorable baby birds: this is just an old wives' tale. Animal mothers are so protective of their offspring that no stink, no matter how gross, would be likely to keep them from caring for their young. More to the point, most birds' sense of smell is as weak as their maternal instinct is strong. A few birds, like parrots and turkey vultures, have a keen olfactory sense, but most backyard birds couldn't smell human scent on their young if their lives depended on it.

So if you come across baby birds without feathers, that means they're still nestlings, and you should do your best to return them to their nest—or, failing that, to jury-rig them a new one. But if you see a young bird *with* feathers, it's a fledgling learning to make its way on its own. Spending a few days flapping around on the ground or a tree branch is totally normal, and its parents are probably nearby, watching over the little guy. You'll probably do more harm than good if you swoop in to help out—but it has nothing to do with your BO.

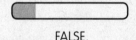

FALSE.

"Don't feed the ducks!"

This one is hard for me to write. As a young child, I fed so many ducks from so many park benches that I now believe my parents were Cold War–era spies. I saw myself as a great benefactor to nature every time I tossed a square of stale Wonder Bread into a mallard-filled pond. But it turns out that ecologically, I was doing a lot more harm than good.

In general, wildlife experts say that it's a bad idea to feed wild animals of any kind—even bird feeders are controversial in some quarters today. I wouldn't go that far, but giving white bread to ducks is a particularly bad idea. In the wild, as a moment's thought will reveal, it's very hard for waterfowl to get hold of bleached, processed flour, so their natural diet consists not of bread but of aquatic plants and bugs. Filling waterfowl up with the kind of stale, non-nutritious treats that most of us bring to a duck pond (bread, popcorn, Fritos) just makes for unhealthy ducks. Often, park ducks get so overfed that the snacks of hundreds of "animal lovers" go uneaten, which can lead to littered shorelines, dangerous mold, and rampant pests. Even if the ducks do manage to choke down all that bread, that just means they produce prodigious amounts of duck poop, polluting ponds and killing off every species except poop-loving algae. In 2011, I read that the city of Lynn, Massachusetts, had filed criminal charges against an eighty-five-year-old woman who'd been feeding ducks in a local city park since the 1960s. That sounded a little draconian to me, until I read the rest of the article. This nice old lady had been bringing full shopping carts of food to the park for years in violation of city warnings, single-handedly turning the pond into a morass of rats and duck poop.

No matter what you feed the animals at the park, it will interfere with their natural feeding and migration behaviors to some degree. It's true that many of the ducks in your local pond are probably so accustomed to human feeding that they now live there year-round, but there's no way to be sure, and your city parks department probably frowns on feeding anyway. If there are no signs posted and you feel you absolutely must feed—and I suppose there's an argument to be made that feeding ducks is one of the few ways city kids get to interact with nature nowadays—at least don't use bread. Britain's Royal Society for the Protection of Birds recommends more nutritious duck-feeding alternatives like fruit, oats, cheese, and potatoes. Make your stale bread into croutons or compost and leave the poor fat ducks out of it.

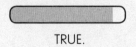

TRUE.

"It's against the law to kill a praying mantis!"

It's certainly a bad idea to kill a praying mantis, since they're such useful garden predators. A mantis can eat its own weight in aphids, beetles, crickets, and mosquitoes *every day*. (They've also been known to trap and eat entire hummingbirds, which is less garden-friendly but still sort of awesome.)

But it's not illegal to kill one, despite over half a century of playground lore to the contrary. Praying mantises (or "mantes," if you're into the whole Greek-plural brevity thing) aren't protected by law anywhere in the United States—not even in Connecticut, where they're the state insect. The international "Red List" that the International Union for Conservation of Nature uses to track threatened animals worldwide lists only one mantis species in trouble: *Apteromantis aptera* of central Spain.

Outside of Iberia, you can slaughter all the praying mantises you want, with no fear of legal recourse. But it's much nicer (and more fun) to make friends with them. Praying mantises can fly when necessary, but they prefer to walk, so they'll march right up your sleeve to your shoulder, given a chance. And keep in mind that the males of the species, at least, are among the few creatures in nature with a good chance at fulfilling every guy's ultimate dream: dying quickly and painlessly during sex. Do you really want to rob them of that possibility?

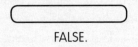

FALSE.

"Quit Eating the Paste!" (School Days)

"Sit up straight, it's good for your back!"

Okay, teachers, I get it. If I were in front of a room full of unruly third graders, I too would want them to be sitting at ramrod-straight attention, like the kids at a Japanese cram school. Nothing would make me want to head to the break room for a quick cigarette like a few rows of hunched-over Quasimodos or kids leaning back lazily like Judd Nelson in *The Breakfast Club*.

But if I were a chiropractor, not a third-grade teacher, I would know to reserve judgment. Doctors and fitness experts now know that the posture that's best for the back is what's called a "neutral spine," which is relaxed and slightly curved, not the ninety-degree L sought by Victorian nannies. The latest OSHA guidelines for computer workstations allow that healthy sitters can choose freely from any of three positions: "upright," "reclined," or "declined." In other words, the exact angle of the back is less important than ergonomic details like keeping your head level and your feet flat on the floor.

A 2006 study at an Aberdeen, Scotland, hospital would go even farther than that. Doctors there took MRI images of healthy patients in three different sitting positions: hunched over, sitting up straight, and leaning back a full 45 degrees. The upright posture actually caused the *most* spinal disc movement, which leads to strain on the back. The radiologists who ran the study ended up endorsing the 135-degree angle (i.e., leaning so far back you look like a sitcom dad watching TV) as the healthiest posture.

Granted, elementary school chairs may not support that level of recline, but it's a good habit for kids to get into if they ever manage to get an office job where the chairs are a little more ergonomic than the blue plastic monstrosities they have to sit on now. In a classroom setting, the best advice is probably for kids to sit at whatever angle of recline keeps the back feeling relaxed and supported, to take breaks for standing and walking as much as possible, and never to sit hunched forward. Hunching puts pressure everywhere from your jaw to your rib cage and, according to a 2009 Ohio State study, actually makes students feel less confident about themselves and their work.

A 2010 MRI study by some orthopedic surgeons at the University of California–San Diego found another growing menace to the vertebrae of the nation's youth: the school backpack. When kids wore heavier backpacks, the study found, their spine curved and discs in their lower back became compressed. Even when the backpack was only 20 percent of the kid's body weight, it caused spinal curvature in about half the subjects. A 10 percent backpack (about nine pounds for the eleven-year-olds in the study) turned out to be much safer.

So don't worry, kids. You're going to hear a lot of crazy stuff about the importance of "posture" for the next few years, but relax. I've got your back.

MOSTLY FALSE.

"Don't sniff the Magic Markers!"

"My name is Ken and I used to really like the smell of rubber cement in junior-high art class."

"Hi, Ken!"

Truthfully, I never felt like my rubber cement enjoyment was a drug problem, but now that I think about it, I'm not sure how I would have defended it to a concerned guidance counselor. "Of course I'm smelling the solvents in an adhesive because the weird smell makes me feel good in a hard-to-define way! But I'm not one of those kids sniffing glue under the bleachers! Because this isn't glue, it's . . . rubber cement!"

Lots of the inhalants that can create brief but euphoric highs can be bought perfectly legally at every grocery store in America: you can huff lighter fluid, paint thinner, shoe polish, even deodorant if you don't mind drugs that smell like "Pacific Surge" or "Wild Musk" or "Grandpa's Undershirt." This can create the perception that inhalants aren't terribly dangerous, which is probably why they're the most widely used drugs (other than alcohol) among young teenagers—more common than cigarettes among seventh graders, according to one 2010 report, and a whopping five times more commonly used than pot. That's a shame, because huffing inhalants can lead to lots of serious health problems: depression, organ damage, seizures, even death. Even a first-time user can fall victim to a rare but potentially fatal form of cardiac arrest called "sudden sniffing death syndrome."

So what about the permanent markers that parents and teachers always told you not to sniff? They contain the same dizzying array of industrial solvents you could find in airplane glues or household cleansers, including (depending on the brand) acetone, butanol, cresols, toluene, and xylene. I don't know of any toxicological research on the seriousness of sniffing Sharpies in particular, but the scientists at the National Institute on Drug Abuse specifically include permanent markers along with other inhalants that can "make you sick, kill your brain cells, and damage your nerves."

In 2008, a Colorado third grader was suspended from school for three days for repeatedly sniffing at a Sharpie stain on his sweatshirt, even when he was asked to stop. There was lots of hubbub about nanny-state overreach, because Sharpies are labeled "nontoxic" and are, in fact, less potent than most commonly abused inhalants. But the school was probably on safe ground: according to the Inhalant Abuse Prevention Program, compulsive sniffing of things like markers and shirtsleeves is a common warning sign of inhalant abuse, and the "nontoxic" label on art supplies doesn't mean that you can't get high off them—it just means that *when used as recommended* (i.e., for drawing, not sniffing) they're not dangerous. Magic Markers didn't get their name from the magical hallucinations they can produce, but it is possible to get, at a minimum, dizzy and light-headed from huffing them. When your kids color, teach them to do as Bill Clinton did and try not to inhale.

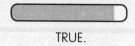

TRUE.

"This will go down on your permanent record!"

"I hope you know that this will go down on your permanent record!" This warning, a standby of sixth-grade social studies teachers everywhere, has such an ominous, Orwellian ring to it that the folk-punk band Violent Femmes borrowed it for the lyrics of their immortal 1983 song "Kiss Off." I always assumed this was a fairly idle threat, the bureaucratic equivalent of writing some troublemaker's name on a chalkboard or even—if necessary!—putting *a check mark* next to it. But teachers are often telling the truth: if you went to a U.S. public school, a detailed record of your life was being kept as far back as kindergarten. And depending on which state you went to school in, that permanent record may still be sitting in a file cabinet somewhere today.

Some of the contents of your primary-school record wouldn't surprise you: it's probably got identifying contact information, academic and attendance records, health and accident reports, aptitude test results, teacher evaluations, and so on. But recent educational initiatives like No Child Left Behind have beefed up the amount of data gathering that school systems do. A 2009 report by Fordham University's Center on Law and Information Policy found that almost half the states now track mental health issues and jail sentences. Other states even keep records of students' Social Security number, pregnancy history, and family financial status.

In 1974, Congress passed the Family Educational Rights and Privacy Act (FERPA, the worst government acronym in the history of bad government acronyms) to protect access to those records, and the law was revised in 2011 to give parents even more control. Still, schools are free to give out "directory information" (basic contact data) freely, and they don't need your consent to share the bulk of your file with other schools, with medical personnel (in an emergency), or with a court (if there's a court order). Military recruiters can see basic information too, unless you opt out. Other requests to see your permanent record require your (or a parent's) consent, and more sensitive parts of your file (information about HIV status, addiction or mental health treatment, or abortion history) must be held to even higher privacy standards.

And just how permanent is your permanent record? Fans of *The Simpsons* may recall the episode in which Bart's friend Milhouse tried to tear up his permanent record, only to have it magically reassemble itself like the Terminator. In reality, FERPA is silent on the amount of time schools can or must keep student records, so state law governs here. In some school districts and states, records get wiped or shredded three years after students leave school. But in other places, permanent records are much more permanent: Illinois law stipulates sixty years, and in other places, schools are instructed to keep them "indefinitely." So your third-grade teacher's pursed-lipped, neatly handwritten account of the time you told the substitute your name was "Hugh G. Rection" may still be moldering in some dusty file cabinet somewhere—but, thanks to FERPA, it's not likely to submarine you in a job interview. Today, we have Facebook for that.

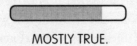

MOSTLY TRUE.

"Your first answer is usually the right one!"

I first heard this advice from Mrs. Nelson in my seventh-grade Study Skills class: if you're torn with doubt over a problem on a multiple-choice test, the first answer you wrote down was probably the right one. It's certainly a confidence-boosting, self-validating piece of advice, since it implies that the right answers are intuitively inside of us all the time, but we sometimes talk ourselves out of them. In other words: you're smarter than you think, so just believe in yourself!

Test-taking guides, even ones from industry leaders like Kaplan, continue to promote this idea as unquestionable dogma. Surveys have found that three-quarters of college students believe the idea, and only 16 percent of Texas A&M faculty members questioned it in a 1984 study. In fact, the issue has been studied academically for over seventy years, and one review found that, out of thirty-three studies, *not a single one* showed that changing answers hurt test-takers. In every kind of test researchers have studied, most student answer changes went from incorrect to correct. In other words, Mrs. Nelson was wrong. If a doubt is niggling at the back of your brain about a test answer as you review it, you should give serious consideration to changing it.

If the evidence is so clear-cut, why are people so convinced that changing answers is a bad idea? In "Counterfactual Thinking and the First Instinct Fallacy," a 2005 article in the *Journal of Personality and Social Psychology*, researchers from Stanford and the University of Illinois uncovered the answer. It's simple: students are *more likely to remember* the times that an answer change worked out badly, because they'll feel cheated by the last-minute switch that cost them the question. Those memories tend to overshadow the (actually much more common) memories of an answer switch that went from incorrect to correct. It's similar, say the authors, to the conviction that all changes of grocery store checkout lane result in slower progress. It's not always true, but we're so outraged by the times when it *is* true that we forget the times when it's not.

I myself can vouch for this kind of self-deluding thinking. In 2004, I was on the quiz show *Jeopardy!* for about six months, so there were dozens of times when I swapped out one answer for another at the last minute. But the only one I really remember was a Final Jeopardy response on one of my last shows. In answer to a clue about the three nations Congress declared war on in the nineteenth century, I quickly wrote down "What are Spain, Mexico, and the UK?" Then, at the last minute, worrying that this was too simple an answer and that there must be some clever trick, I swapped out Britain for the Confederacy just in time for the think music to end. My original answer, it turned out, had been right. That little brain fart didn't lose me the game, but it did cost me over $18,000. I'm sure there were plenty of times I switched from a wrong answer to a right one at the last minute, but, tellingly, I can't think of a single one right now.

FALSE.

"Chew on your pencil and you'll get lead poisoning!"

You probably already know that pencil "lead" isn't actually lead: it's graphite and clay, and graphite is just carbon, which is also what you are made out of unless you are some kind of *Star Trek* alien or sentient computer. So it's not dangerous in any way. In fact, pencils have *never* been made out of real lead. When graphite was first discovered in Borrowdale, England, in 1564, nobody knew what the shiny, black, perfect-for-writing stuff was, so somebody decided to call it plumbago, or "black lead."

That said, teachers warning pencil-chewers about the dangers of lead actually were right—until 1978, anyway, when the United States banned lead in household paint. In general, the EPA says that leaded paint doesn't pose a danger as long as it's in good condition, but if paint starts to chip or get sanded to dust, that's when kids ingest or inhale it, which can lead to serious developmental problems. A 1971 report by the Health Services and Mental Health Administration found that some brands of pencil contained as much as a microgram of lead in their deceptively cheerful outer yellow paint. According to the study's authors, that's enough to accumulate in the tissues of a child eating one-fifth of a pencil's worth of paint a day—an aggressive pencil-chewing rate, to be sure, but not impossible. Lead chromate isn't saliva-soluble but it will dissolve in stomach acid, so the whole issue, the authors sternly pointed out, hinges on how much painted wood actually makes it into the chewer and how much just winds up on the classroom floor.

Nowadays, of course, the yellow paint is lead free and the point is moot. So toxicologists don't care anymore if you chew your pencil—but your dentist might, since pencil chewing can screw up your bite, not to mention causing tooth abrasion and gum trauma. But on the plus side, you'll have a desk full of spitty, disgusting Ticonderoga No. 2s that look like they were owned by a family of beavers, and no one will ever want to steal your pencils. So there are arguments on both sides.

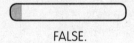

FALSE.

"Just ignore bullies and they'll leave you alone!"

Parents are in a bind when it comes to advising kids on bullying. If you say, "Just sock the bully in the jaw!" you're raising a thuggish hooligan. If you say, "Tell a teacher right away next time," you're raising a weaselly little snitch. If you say, "Just defuse the situation with charisma and humor"—well, any kid socially adept enough to do that probably isn't getting bullied in the first place. So it's easy to see why many confused parents fall back on this incredibly lame standby: "Just ignore it, and they'll probably stop." Subtext: "I have no idea how to solve your problem, which makes me uncomfortable."

Often, the "just ignore it" advice springs from a fundamental misconception about bullies: that they needle their targets out of boredom, and if they can't get a rise out of one doormat, they'll move on to another. This may be true of why siblings tease or fight with each other, but it's terrible advice for the classroom. A 2010 study out of the Netherlands showed that bullies are actually incredibly tactical about how they pick their targets: they carefully (and accurately, in most cases) choose the kids who are already unpopular with their same-gender peers, so they can bully at will without losing the respect of their in-group. It seems clear from these results that the purpose of most bullying is to secure status and avoid resistance of any kind. So bullies don't pick on a classmate in hopes of getting a reaction. Quite the contrary: they bully *in hopes of getting no reaction at all.*

This is a crucial realization, because it points out why "Just ignore it" is, in many cases, the worst possible advice. Bullies are looking for the path of least resistance, and many will interpret silence as acquiescence: they got away with it, they "won," they'll come back for more the next time they need peer validation. In 2012, the Youth Voice Project surveyed over thirteen thousand kids about bullying. Ignoring a bully was found to be one of the least effective coping tactics listed—22 percent of the time, it actually made things worse. "There are times when doing nothing makes sense—for example, if the bully is older or you're in an unsupervised area," social worker Patricia Kelley Criswell agrees in *The Christian Science Monitor,* "but overall, with repeated bullying, ignoring isn't an effective strategy."

So what does work? Telling someone—a parent, a teacher, or a friend—worked in up to 38 percent of all cases. If we're going to make inroads against the bullying epidemic, old-fashioned adults will need to get past their instinct that seeking adult help is "tattling," that it's bad form in some way. When you think about it, there's something almost perverse about insisting that kids "solve their own problems," even if they're problems so serious that even mature adults would never try to solve them alone. If you were getting relentlessly and cruelly hassled at work, you'd get fed up at some point and talk to your boss or HR, right? If it happened on the street, you'd eventually look for a cop, right? Those aren't dishonorable solutions, and by the same token, kids should be able to count on classmates and adults to help them shut down bullying at school.

Unless you think "Just ignore it and it'll go away" is a good strategy for other life problems—ignore your bills, ignore your health issues, ignore family problems—don't confuse your kids by imposing it on them in the classroom. Life almost always gets better after bullying, the It Gets Better Project reminds us. But when kids learn smart coping strategies—standing up for themselves, enlisting peers to help, confiding in adults—it can get better a lot quicker.

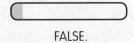

FALSE.

"Don't draw on your skin, you'll get blood poisoning!"

I was a chronic ballpoint doodler as a kid, and not always on paper. The back of your hand, I learned, was the best place to write down phone numbers and homework assignments—the palm wears off too fast, so that's the place for more transitory distractions: spaceships, sharks, and the like. The side of the hand, where the thumb meets the index finger, was reserved for little talking faces, à la ventriloquist Señor Wences. S'aright? S'aright.

Somehow, my fairly benign take on body modification managed to fly under adult radar until seventh grade, when a science teacher noticed the Bic masterpiece on my right forearm (not drawn by me that day, as it happened, but by the cute Asian girl in the seat next to me) and brought class to a screeching halt. Literally, she screeched. Inks are toxic, they can cause cancer, they'll get into my bloodstream and poison me, and so on. I was shocked. I'd been courting death by blood poisoning all these years and never knew it?

It's okay, aspiring body artists: ballpoint ink isn't going to kill you. The National Institutes of Health does include "ink poisoning" on its list of first aid emergencies, but notes that "because writing ink is generally considered nonpoisonous, recovery is very likely." That's because "large amounts of writing ink must be consumed (more than an ounce) before treatment is needed." An ounce? Wow. That's over a hundred ballpoint pens' worth of ink, and all in one big oral dose. There's not even a mention of transdermal absorption, which would deliver much, much less of any toxin—but, to be fair, would put it straight into the bloodstream. But water-based inks, the kind found in ballpoint pens, are so safe it doesn't really matter.

As we've seen, the ingredient list for permanent markers is a little iffier and sometimes includes slightly toxic solvents like xylene. Sanford, the company that makes Sharpies, hedges on the question of skin use, telling customers, "Although the markers have been tested and are safe for art use by children and adults, we express caution and do not suggest using Sharpie markers on skin." But come on, who are they kidding? Forty percent of young Americans now have tattoos, and keep in mind that that's a much larger dose of ink, of a type completely unregulated by the Food and Drug Administration, injected *directly into* skin tissue and left there for years. I'm not saying every tattoo is a great idea (I'm looking at you, barista with the Bon Iver lyrics on your wrist!), but I haven't noticed some blood-poisoning epidemic as a result. By comparison, the idea that you could get sick from a minuscule bit of much safer ink temporarily left on the surface of the skin—well, it's exceedingly unlikely. Señor Wences lived to be 103, you know.

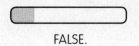

FALSE.

"Kids These Days!"
(Technology and Modern Life)

"Keep the fork out of the toaster or you'll get zapped!"

Your mom was right to freak out when she saw you trying to rescue a stuck Pop-Tart using a butter knife. Toasters, even today, are fairly simple contraptions, heating bread via, essentially, a controlled short circuit. Nichrome (nickel and chromium) wire is wrapped around a heating element, usually a sheet of the fireproof mineral mica, and a few amps of current are run through it. Resistance in the wire is high enough that the filaments start to glow red-hot, which toasts the bread.

Jabbing a big piece of conductive metal into live, exposed wires is, obviously, problematic, and for much of the twentieth century, toaster electrocution was a not-unheard-of way to die. Your parents no doubt read these news stories, many of which involved children, and thus was their toaster-safety outlook fixed for the rest of their lives. But modern safety technology is helping to short-circuit evolution by making it much harder to die via toaster idiocy. Most kitchen outlets today have devices called ground fault circuit interrupters built into them, which can detect a dangerous current imbalance (because current is heading somewhere it shouldn't, like up your fork and arm, for example) and trip the switch before you get zapped.

But nothing is foolproof. Americans still went to the emergency room 354 times in 2010 for toaster-related injuries. Most of those cases were burns, but doctors' notes show that about one in ten was an electric shock. So plenty of people are still contending with faulty toasters or faulty wiring or both. If you want to be extra-safe, assume the worst: the outlet might be wired backward, for example, or you might accidentally hit the on/off switch while you're rooting around. Even be careful with wooden implements or when the toaster is unplugged: your poking around could damage the heating element (mica is fairly brittle) or cause a short circuit between the wiring and the toaster's metal frame. You won't get a shock immediately, but next time you plug in, you could be toast.

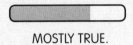

MOSTLY TRUE.

"Don't yank the plug out of the wall like that!"

This was a constant bugaboo of the parents of a friend of mine: electrical plugs had to be removed directly from the wall by hand, never yanked out by the cord. In my mind's eye, I pictured the apocalyptic consequences of unplugging the "wrong way": a lightninglike arc of electricity following the vacuum cleaner plug as it spun delicately through the air, followed by an earsplitting crack and, presumably, every light in the house and maybe the neighborhood going out at once. It seemed pretty awesome.

The truth is much less dramatic. You probably won't cause any pyrotechnics by yanking a cord from the wall, but you might damage the cord or the outlet. If the housing is plugged tightly into the wall socket, it may not come loose immediately when pulled. Instead, you might just pull insulation or wiring out at the end of the cord, bend the plug prongs, or spread the tension clips inside the outlet.

There's an argument to be made that, for safety reasons, *all* plugs should pull effortlessly from the wall, to avoid people and appliances taking spills when someone trips on a cord. Apple's patented MagSafe power connectors attach magnetically, so they pull out safely when tugged on, straining no wires or connectors. In the future, breakaway cords like this could make it okay to yank out the power cords of our electric flying cars and robot maids. But for now, you're still going to have to walk *all the way over* to the outlet, sigh, and pull on the housing.

TRUE.

"Start saving now and compound interest will make you rich!"

More than two hundred years ago, a Welsh philosopher named Richard Price discovered compound interest for the first time, and his eyes turned into dollar signs, literally, like a Scrooge McDuck comic. (There may also have been a cash-register sound; history does not relate.) He wrote, "One penny, put out at our Savior's birth to five percent compound interest, would, in the present year 1781, have increased to a greater sum than would be contained in *two hundred millions* of Earths, all solid gold. But, if put out to simple interest, it would, in the same time, have amounted to no more than *seven shillings and sixpence.*"

Two hundred million times the mass of the Earth in gold sounds nice, but where would you put it? Still, Price's math was solid, and Benjamin Franklin, writing his will later that decade, decided to try a real-life experiment of the compounding principle. Upon his death, he set aside £1,000 for the cities of Boston and Philadelphia—but with the caveat that they couldn't touch the money for a century and would not get all of it for *two* centuries. Sure enough, when the one hundredth anniversary of Franklin's death rolled around, Boston and Philly received half a million dollars for public works projects, and by

1990, when Franklin's long experiment finally ended, the cities had rebuilt their funds to a total of seven million dollars.

Stories like this are often used to explain to schoolchildren the magical-seeming powers of "compound interest." To review: simple interest means that, at designated intervals, you earn an additional percentage on the original amount of money you invested somewhere. But with compound interest, the rate is calculated against the original amount invested *plus any new interest earned since.* For the first few years, the difference is barely noticeable, but the growing principal gradually turns the investment into an unstoppable express train of savings.

This is true, as far as it goes, and it's a good way to get kids excited about saving their allowance instead of immediately blowing it on candy and Chinese-made dollar-store crap. It also works to get new college grads more serious about saving, if they see there's a substantial difference between the retirement power of a dollar saved at age twenty-five versus one saved at forty-five.

But my beef with compound interest is that people still explain it using impossibly dated examples and, therefore, overpromise on the amazing results of compounding. If you were in fifth grade in the late 1970s, interest rates might have been as high as 20 percent, which no doubt made investment examples seem pretty awesome. If we use the "Rule of 72" shortcut for compound interest (divide the number 72 by your interest rate to find the amount of time it would take your money to double), then you could double your 1979 investment in just three and a half years! (Well, if you ignore the early 1980s recession.) The story problems from my childhood tended to use interest rates around 6 percent (double your money in just over a decade!) or the historical stock market return rate, around 10 percent (double every seven years!)

But let's fast-forward to today, with interest rates hovering around 1 or 2 percent with no reason to think that will change drastically any time soon. Compound interest still works in today's economic climate, of course—but a 1 percent interest rate means that if you invest $1,000 today and compound it annually, in twenty years, you'll have . . . $1,220. Wow. Not exactly the eye-popping numbers you remember from your middle-school money management class, right? And let's not forget inflation: your $1,220 will have less buying power in twenty years than it does today, due to rising prices. Even when interest rates were at their highest, around 1980, inflation was also peaking at 13 percent or so. In fact, there haven't been too many times in the last century when your rate of return from traditional investments like savings accounts and CDs would outpace inflation at all. It's quite possible to *lose* money via the Miracle of Compounding!

Computer-programmer-turned-cartoonist Randall Munroe noted this problem in a much-circulated 2011 installment of his nerdy webcomic xkcd. "So compound interest isn't some magical force," one character concludes in the final panel, after running some numbers. "Yeah, I'm just gonna try to make more money," says the other. This got me thinking: when we teach our kids about compound interest, are we teaching them about thrift, like we think, or are we teaching them that the universe will automatically accumulate money for them in some mystical fashion their whole lives, regardless of their earning power? Given the uncertainties of investing today, we might want to *also* emphasize that the best way to make money is probably *a career that will make money,* and (most importantly) spending less of it than you earn.

Sorry, kids: compound interest doesn't mean you'll be living in a Richie Rich cartoon at forty and watching your butler light fires with hundred-dollar bills. The man on those bills, Benjamin Franklin, may have been an early believer in compound interest, but even he had his doubts. "Considering the accidents to which all human affairs and projects are subject in such a length of time," he wrote, "I have, perhaps, too much flattered myself with a vain fancy that these dispositions, if carried into execution, will be continued without interruption and have the effects proposed." Compound interest might work, but Ben was right: due to "the accidents to which all human affairs and projects are subject," it's no magic bullet.

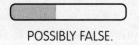

POSSIBLY FALSE.

"Don't flick the light switches off and on, it wastes money!"

Kids love playing with light switches (thunder noises optional). Parents hate it and yell at them. It's one of the eternal struggles of the universe—I think I saw a nature documentary about it.

Obviously, turning a light on and off repeatedly is going to eat more electricity and bulb life than leaving it off. The more interesting comparison is between a light that's on for, say, one minute uninterrupted, and a light that's on for a minute *total* amid two minutes of kiddie switch-flicking. Do they use the same chunk of electric bill and lightbulb-shopping bill, or not?

If the bulbs are fluorescent, the outcome isn't particularly close. Fluorescent lighting requires a brief but very high "inrush" current to start up. This initial blast of current lasts only half a cycle, one hundred-twentieth of a second, but depending on the type of electronic ballast in the lamp, it can use electricity at over a hundred times the rate of normal light operation. Because you have to balance the costs of electricity (which are lowered by leaving the light on) and bulb replacement (which are lowered by turning the light off), the exact tipping point will depend on utility rates in your area, but the Department of Energy recommends a rule of thumb between five and fifteen minutes. If you're going to be out of the room longer than that, turn the light off. If not, it's actually more cost-effective to leave it on. (Suffice it to say, most kid light-flipping happens at a much faster interval than five to fifteen minutes.)

The math is different with old-fashioned incandescent bulbs, because they're both less expensive to buy and less efficient to use (fully 90 percent of the electricity running an incandescent bulb is producing heat, not light). As a result, the Department of Energy recommends turning these lights off any time they're not in use, no matter how short the interval. But if you're interested in prolonging bulb life, yes, there's a brief "inrush current" period for incandescents as well.

And because the highest currents and temperatures occur immediately after a bulb is switched on, that's when the most stress is put on the tungsten-wire filament inside. You've probably noticed that bulbs tend to burn out at the moment they're switched on and not when they've been on for hours, right? That's because the high temperatures at switch-on can melt the parts of the filament that have been thinned and weakened by long hours of use. Flipping a light switch on and off presumably makes that wear happen faster, and it can definitely accelerate that "last straw" moment when the bulb finally burns out.

Compared to other things you can do to make your home more energy-efficient (attic insulation, newer furnace and appliances, turning down the heat at night), switch flipping is just rounding error, a few bucks a year no matter how inefficient your kids' bulb use is. But hey, you asked.

TRUE.

"Don't mix different types of batteries!"

"Do not mix old and new batteries," says the official Duracell list of frequently asked battery questions. It goes on to denounce battery mixing with the fervor of a 1960s Southern segregationist governor. "Different batteries are designed for different purposes. Mixing a lithium battery with an alkaline battery will not improve device performance. . . . Do not mix different battery brands within a device."

You'll forgive me, I hope, for raising a skeptical eyebrow when I read that. Of course Duracell's packaging wants you to stick to one kind of battery—if you're reading their literature, it's probably going to be theirs! By the same token, they know you'll buy more batteries if you always have to replace an entire device's worth of batteries, rather than swapping them out one by one. I'll admit: I doubted the wisdom of Duracell.

But Duracell and your parents were right: mixing batteries is bad news, as ill-advised as mixing beer and wine, religion and politics, or dating and Craigslist. If one battery in a device has a stronger cell than the other, due to brand or age or type or whatever, it may overheat rapidly in an attempt to compensate for the other, underperforming one. (This can happen in relationships too, but I digress.) The Department of Energy's health and safety office reported in 2008 that an employee at Oak Ridge National Laboratory mixed two different brands of lithium battery—one with a vent safety feature design, one without—in a flashlight. The flashlight spontaneously combusted, charring both the worker and his shirt pocket. Oak Ridge being a nuclear facility, this accident was taken very seriously, but I assume you'd want to avoid the same kind of inferno in your home's toys and remote controls.

But I still question my mother's omniscience (I call it "Momniscience") when it comes to batteries, for one reason: to this day, she keeps them in her fridge behind the condiments, insisting that the cold storage helps their charge last longer. The folks at Duracell say that putting their batteries on ice "is not necessary or recommended," and their counterparts at Energizer go farther than that, claiming that it's downright harmful, because the condensation when a refrigerated battery warms back up can damage its shell or corrode the contacts. Additionally, a battery won't perform well when it's straight from the crisper, for the same reason that your car has a hard time starting on a wintry morning. Product tests do reveal a slight advantage for chilled alkaline batteries in very, very long-term storage (after five years, refrigerated batteries kept 93 percent of their charge compared to 90 percent for those in room-temperature storage), but I tend to agree with the manufacturers: that tiny edge isn't worth the risk that your batteries will struggle or corrode when they come in from the cold.

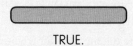

TRUE.

"Never run the microwave empty!"

Short answer: it depends. "Some ovens should not be operated when empty," says the Food and Drug Administration. "Refer to the instruction manual for your oven."

There's nothing dangerous *to you* about running an empty microwave—you're not going to gain superpowers or become your own night-light or anything—but it might be dangerous to the microwave itself. As we saw on page 150, a microwave interior is metal lined, to prevent the microwave radiation from getting out and wandering around your kitchen. But that also means that the waves will keep reflecting off these walls and around the cooking chamber until something (food, generally) absorbs them. If there are no pizza bites in there to absorb any energy, the waves will continue to bounce around like SuperBalls, getting the wrong stuff hot. The glass turntable might melt, or if there's even the tiniest of sharp metal edges anywhere in the cooking cavity, you could get a blowtorchlike electric arc and then a big fire. (Your parents were *also* right about metal in the microwave. Don't leave any silverware on your plate.) Most commonly, the energy will reenter the waveguide where it came from and overheat your magnetron, the doohickey that turns electricity into microwaves. Result: dead oven.

Most new microwaves have a fuse or thermostat to prevent this very thing, which will shut off the oven before the magnetron gets zapped. So your microwave may be perfectly safe. But any oven new enough to have a safety shutoff is certain to have a timer, so there's no reason to use an empty microwave as an expensive egg timer anymore. I know, I mostly stick to the "Add 30 Seconds" button too, but there are like fifteen others. Try fiddling around with them; they must do *something*.

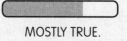

MOSTLY TRUE.

"Keep your arms inside the car, that's dangerous!"

I'll admit: I really wanted this one to be false. What's more fun on childhood car trips than sticking your hand into the wind tunnel outside and feeling that cool freeway blast on your soft, hairless skin? Maybe your hand is Superman, or a fighter jet, or a majestic bald eagle. There can't really be that many accidents that result from people sticking their limbs out of cars, can there?

Actually, there can. "Sideswipe injury," a.k.a. "traffic elbow," is such a common form of upper-body trauma that it often gets its own section in medical textbooks. These injuries are typically caused when a driver is resting his or her left elbow (or right elbow, in right-hand drive countries) outside an open car window at the moment the car is sideswiped by an oncoming car, or, less commonly, when a driver loses control and collides with a stationary object like a tree or post. The results range from serious skin abrasions, serious enough for massive blood loss to be a concern, all the way up to compound fractures, the disturbingly named condition "floating elbow," and even amputation.

The quintessential urban-legend version of this nightmare, the school-bus-window decapitation, has never actually happened, though at least four U.S. kids have died of school bus injuries in recent years when their heads slammed into trees and poles. (The times when kids on the bus are most likely to have their heads out of the window—calling to friends getting on or off—are, tragically, the same times that the bus is most likely to be passing closest to poles and tree branches.)

Most of the medical literature on sideswipe injuries, I'll grant you, comes from a generation or two ago, when cars were smaller, roads were narrower, and more drivers left their windows open on a hot day because they didn't have air-conditioning. But a 2006 report out of Australia suggests that even in that country, where driving with your elbow out is explicitly illegal, a hospital might still see an injury like this every month or two, and that nearly all require surgery. "Increased awareness of the problem and further recommendations to keep arms within the vehicle" were cited as the most important factors to "decrease the incidence of this frequently devastating but easily prevented injury."

You might argue that kids have shorter arms and are less likely to *leave* them hanging out a car window the way a driver might, but if you look at the numbers, you'll see that kids aren't the best judges of car window safety. According to the National Highway Traffic Safety Administration, about a thousand children are injured by power windows each year, and five actually die. In a typical accident, a child accidentally leans or kneels on a power window button with some body part sticking out the window; when it's the child's head, he or she may choke to death. Nonprofit groups have been lobbying for years to have automakers install automatic-reverse sensors on power windows, but so far only 20 percent of new cars have the feature. At least all U.S. cars must now have lever-style switches in place of rocker or toggle ones, so you can't close a window by mashing it down accidentally.

So it may be super-annoying when your kids play with the power windows (*"Cut that out, it's bad for the car!"*), but it turns out there are also plenty of safety reasons for that driver-side power window override switch, and keeping kids' arms and legs inside the ride at all times is certainly one of them. I think I might still allow my kids the occasional Superman moment on the open road, but I'll be picking my spots pretty carefully.

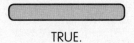

TRUE.

"Well, Life **Isn't** Fair!"
(The Motivational Mom)

"You are a special little snowflake!"

What would the holiday season be without children folding squares of typing paper into eighths or sixteenths and then cutting them into elaborate doilies vaguely resembling snow crystals, to be hung from drop-ceiling tiles in a school classroom? Said children have probably been reassured since birth that they themselves are "special little snowflakes"—that is, as endlessly different and unique as the crystalline lattices that condense from the sky during a winter storm.

Well, the children may be unique, but the snowflakes sure aren't. The old adage about snowflake uniqueness dates back to Wilson Bentley, a turn-of-the-century Vermont man so fascinated by snowflakes that he spent his life perfecting a process to photograph these miraculous "ice blossoms," as he called them. In a series of journal articles, Bentley argued that no two snowflakes are alike, an idea convincingly illustrated by his six-thousand-photograph collection of beautiful snowflake images.

At a molecular level, of course, Bentley was right. There are something like a sextillion molecules of water in a tiny snowflake, and the arrangement of hydrogen and oxygen isotopes within those water molecules will never be precisely duplicated. But at a more meaningful level—that of microscopic inspection—Bentley was wrong. The simplest possible snowflake shapes, seen in the smallest flakes that fall shortly after condensation, are repeated all the time. In 1988, a government researcher named Nancy Knight produced two snowflakes that had fallen during the same Wisconsin snowstorm. Their shapes—simple hexagonal prisms—were identical, no matter how closely she looked.

So we need a better metaphor for the specialness of our children—snowflakes have been out since 1988. I suggest "UPC codes."

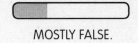

MOSTLY FALSE.

"We only use 10 percent of our brains, you know!"

It's mystifying to me how this completely invented factoid—sort of an insulting one, when you think about it—has become such a self-help standby. I suppose the implication is one of untapped potential: Buck up, you're capable of so much more than you think! Ten times more, say unnamed neuroscientists!

This idea probably seeped into the public consciousness in 1936, via Lowell Thomas's foreword to the bajillion-selling book *How to Win Friends and Influence People*. Thomas was a writer and broadcaster best known for making a media star out of T. E. Lawrence (the Arthur Kennedy character in the film *Lawrence of Arabia* is based on Thomas), but he also introduced the world to the motivational ideas of his former business manager Dale Carnegie. He wrote in his introduction, "Professor William James of Harvard used to say that the average person develops only 10 percent of his latent mental ability." Carnegie's book sold fifteen million copies containing that quote, and a myth was born.

It's true that William James did make lofty claims about how we "use only a small part of our possible mental and physical resources," but he never put a percentage to it. This statement is almost certainly true in a general way: of course, most people achieve less in life than it is theoretically possible for them to. But that's just human nature, not some built-in limitation of brain anatomy, as Thomas teetered perilously close to suggesting and his readers have since taken as established fact.

In psychology professor Barry Beyerstein's 1999 essay "Whence Cometh the Myth that We Use Only 10% of Our Brains?," Beyerstein offers a meticulously thorough seven-point takedown of this misconception. His most compelling evidence comes from modern brain-imaging technologies and studies of patients with brain damage. MRI tests and positron-emission tomography didn't exist in William James's day, but today, it's quite possible to see which parts of the brain we use for what functions. Even when we're asleep, says Beyerstein, all areas of the brain are active. Serious damage has to be present for *any* part of the brain, much less 90 percent, to go completely dark. And Beyerstein points out that even slight damage to pretty much any area of the brain can cause drastic impairment. If 90 percent of the brain was just excess meat, you'd think it would be possible to drill all kinds of holes in it and not even notice.

We know what happens to brain cells that aren't used: we can look at them with microscopes and watch them atrophy. The fact that this isn't happening to nine-tenths of your brain right now means that evolution has engineered your brain to be as efficient and compact as it has every other part of your body: it's almost all in use almost all of the time. Granted, the brain is quite good at redundancy and can find miraculous-seeming workarounds when part of it is injured, in ways we still don't understand well. But that doesn't mean the vast majority of it goes unused—you wouldn't say you use only 50 percent of your kidneys just because you could live without one if necessary.

In a way, it's sad that we don't have this vast untapped reservoir of gray matter up our cerebral sleeve. Presumably that would be the part of the brain that could perform astounding mental calculations, or Sherlock Holmes–like feats of deduction, or telekinesis. It's fun to imagine that someday we could just flex the right mental muscle and gain superpowers, like unlocking a video game achievement. But you know what? In science fiction, when characters suddenly super-evolve, they immediately turn evil as well, and usually start speaking in a big reverb-y voice. Maybe it's a *good* thing that all our mental potential is pretty much tapped.

FALSE.

"These are the best years of your life—enjoy them!"

A perverse but apparently crucial part of parenthood is constantly reminding your kids how good they have it. Now that I have kids, I totally understand this impulse. The first time a kid whines, "Do I have to do *everything* around here?" as he slides off the couch after an hour of dull-eyed TV watching just because you told him to collect his socks in the middle of the floor—well, something snaps inside you and you're never the same again. But there's a fine line between reminding kids to be grateful for their blessings ("When I was your age, I had to walk to school uphill in the snow!") and becoming the bitter alcoholic mom from an after-school special ("I hope you have a kid *just like you* someday!").

There have been decades of research on the relationship between age and happiness, and the trend is pretty clear: college-aged kids are very happy, and so are the elderly. In the West, happiness reaches its lowest point around the traditional midlife crisis age, forty-five or so. Since the 1990s, researchers have called this trend "the U-bend" and tend to credit the senior-citizen rebound to the clarity that comes with age. In your eighties, you're no longer struggling to get ahead or imagining some illusory future happiness. You're probably watching friends and family pass away, and that teaches you, perhaps for the first time, to be content in the moment.

Few of these studies include children, probably because the happiness of a nine-year-old ("I won a Pokémon battle!") and the happiness of an adult ("It's not cancer!") are in many ways apples and oranges. But a landmark 2012 study by the Children's Society, a British nonprofit, surveyed over thirty thousand kids and found that just 9 percent reported "low levels of subjective well-being," i.e., feeling unhappy, at any given time. This was reported as a sad and shocking statistic, but it actually looks pretty good when you stack it up against adult numbers. When a 2009 Gallup Poll asked adults a similar question ("Did you experience happiness or enjoyment a lot of the day yesterday?"), 20 percent of college-aged people said no, and that number got as high as 40 percent as it neared the buying-a-sports-car nadir of the U-bend.

The science-of-happiness studies come with lots of philosophical disagreements over the value of what is actually being measured. For example, these studies *always* demonstrate that having kids around, no matter how old, is a great way to lower your net happiness. And yet, when the average parent is asked about child rearing, they frame it as the highlight of their lives. It's possible that happiness is a less meaningful goal for adults than things like having meaning or purpose. But as far as the numbers can tell us, yes, children are a good deal happier than adults, and even slightly happier than old people. But you don't have to remind them all the time that it's all downhill from here.

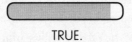

TRUE.

"It's okay, even Einstein flunked math!"

I'm not sure why parents are so eager to inform their kids that Einstein was bad at math, because (spoiler alert!) Einstein is widely known to have been a talented guy at equations and whatnot. Presumably the idea is to convince academic underachievers that they may just be late bloomers like Einstein, sort of like telling young would-be sports stars that Michael Jordan was cut from his high school basketball team. (That one is an urban legend, too, though it's true that Jordan didn't make the varsity team until his junior year.)

The problem with this homily is that we need a better life example, because Einstein was a spectacular math student in his youth. He laughed in 1935 when a Princeton rabbi showed him a *Ripley's Believe It or Not* cartoon claiming that he had bad grades as a child. "I never failed in mathematics," he replied. "Before I was fifteen I had mastered differential and integral calculus." In fact, Einstein was so far ahead of his peers that he was largely self-taught, out of advanced texts his parents bought him. At the age of eleven, he worked out his own novel proof of the Pythagorean Theorem, which seems to be pretty good evidence that he was, as my kids' teachers say in parent conferences, "working at or above grade level."

At his Munich high school, Einstein did learn that languages weren't his thing—too mechanical, he thought, and he said he had a "bad memory" for text. And yet he aced every class. In 1929, when Einstein was fifty, the headmaster of his old school got so tired of hearing the "Einstein flunked" rumors that he actually produced his old pupil's childhood report card, and sure enough, his grades were excellent. There seems to be no truth to the old story about the future physicist's Latin teacher repeatedly telling him, "You'll never amount to anything, Einstein!" (But I bet Einstein wondered if people were being sarcastic dicks every time they called him by his last name. "You forgot your coffee mug, Einstein!" "Nice proof, Einstein!" Just one of the hazards of the job, I guess.)

Kids who struggle with math may or may not grow up to be scientists or engineers. In many cases, a low math grade is probably a sign that it's not a particular strength and they should be focusing on other talents. But if you want to use Einstein as an object lesson for kids, it's his language-learning skill that's more interesting than his math prowess: he wasn't great at it, but he worked hard and got good grades anyway. Nice report card, Einstein.

FALSE.

"Your name just makes you more special!"

In 2011, *The New York Times* reported on the shocking new trend of *parents giving their kids weird-ass names*! Have you heard of this thing? I'm just kidding, of course you have. My wife and I got many disapproving looks when we named our daughter Caitlin, spelled the old-fashioned Irish way. What a missed opportunity to name her something *unique*: Katelyn, Caytlin, Keétlein, Qait-linn, Chääyaiett*Lynne. Laura Wattenberg, author of *The Baby Name Wizard*, told the *Times* that Google is the tool of choice for most of today's brave name pioneers: "Parents thinking of a baby name will type it in and say: 'Oh, no, it's taken. There are already three others with that name.'" Someday soon every single baby name will be like "Qaddafi": impossible to spell right, impossible to spell wrong.

Some interesting new research by Dr. David Figlio, a University of Florida economics professor, points out that treating baby naming like a personal creativity exercise assigned by your yoga teacher may have long-term consequences for the real victim here: the child. In his 2006 study "Boys Named Sue," Figlio examined boys given names that are more common nowadays for girls: Ashley, Shannon, Courtney, and so on. The study is named for the Johnny Cash song about a man who says, "I grew up quick and I grew up mean, my fist got hard and my wits got keen," because of all the fights his effeminate name caused. Sure enough, Figlio discovered, boys with "girly"-sounding names did indeed, when they hit middle-school age, end up struggling academically and disrupting class more than their peers, especially if there was a girl in the class who shared their name. (Ouch!)

The previous year, Figlio had published an even more ingenious study: he compared kids using the Scrabble scores of their names. (As fans of the game will recall, longer words or words full of unusual letters earn the highest point totals.) Figlio was able to demonstrate that the bigger a Scrabble bonanza your child's name is, the worse he will do on math and reading tests during his school career. You might complain that correlation does not equal causation and that Figlio's Scrabble-mouthful kids were struggling due to intervening variables like class or race. But not so! He ingeniously compared kids with lower-scoring names to their vowel-challenged *siblings* and was still able to observe a statistical difference, which he chalked up to teachers subconsciously giving less-favorable treatment to kids with unusual names.

"Name your kids what you love, but be aware there are consequences," Figlio told the *Times*. These studies do have disturbing implications related to class and race in America, but I can think of at least one silver lining: the spoiled, whimsically named children of celebrities are finally going to get their comeuppance in junior high.

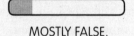

MOSTLY FALSE.

"If you're mad, just go let off some steam!"

"Don't bottle it up!" we warn kids about anger, apparently under the misconception that they are little pneumatic machines or balloon animals of some kind. "Let off steam! Vent! Get that off your chest!" Aristotle was singing the virtues of "catharsis"—the healthy purging of emotion via art—three centuries before Christ, but it was Sigmund Freud who applied Aristotle's idea to psychology. Freud was convinced that negative emotions would lead to mental illnesses like hysteria if they weren't released in controlled ways. His ideas have seeped out into popular culture to such a degree that we nod wisely when self-help gurus tell us to deal with frustration by going outside and yelling our heads off or whaling on a punching bag. Without Freud, we wouldn't have "primal scream" therapy or its many variants, like pillow-pounding anger-management classes and "Destructotherapy," a new stress-relief fad from northern Spain in which participants have two hours to bash up a junkyard with sledgehammers while heavy metal music blares.

In general, Freud had a point: people tend to be happier and healthier when they express their emotions rather than keeping them hidden. But anger and aggression are an interesting case: they tend to be contagious, for one thing, so it only takes one short fuse to turn an otherwise contented room (or household) into a rage cage. But more to the point, there's now over fifty years of evidence that venting actually makes the venter feel worse as well! In a landmark 1959 study, a group of subjects was insulted, and then half were given nails to hammer into a block of wood. The authors expected the cathartic hammering to make those subjects less hostile and were surprised to find them notably *more* hostile afterward. In 1973, Dr. Albert Bandura, often called the world's greatest living psychiatrist, issued a statement disavowing catharsis theory, since venting "may inadvertently reinforce aggressive tendencies." Subsequent experiments have found that any "steam blowing" behavior—even physical exercise like going for a run—will keep an angry person's arousal levels high. And that makes them more likely to turn aggressive, even if they say they believe in venting or self-report feeling better afterward.

That's probably the reason people cling to their stress-relief pillows and punching bags: it might make them feel a little better in the short term, even if it doesn't reduce their hostility or solve the underlying problem. This isn't just an academic issue, either: it's at the core of the debate over whether violent video games are healthy (they help us purge our dark side so we don't steal cars or shoot up Soviet nerve gas laboratories in real life!) or harmful (they teach us that violence solves problems and makes us more aggressive in real life!). There's still no academic consensus here; even scholarly reviews of the very same literature often come to different conclusions. But when it comes to real-life venting, psychologists are now pretty sure that it does no good and often makes us feel worse. The right approach with kids is the exact opposite—help them cope in more relaxing ways: deep breaths, counting to ten, communication, problem solving. Granted, these strategies aren't as cinematic as the kind of anger management we learn from movies (Captain Kirk yelling "*Khaaaan!*" on a barren meteorite, the *Office Space* guys bashing a finicky laser printer to bits), but they definitely satisfy a more important life rule: WWMRD? That is, "What Would Mr. Rogers Do?"

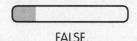

FALSE.

"What If Your Friends All Jumped off a Cliff?" (The Awkward Age)

"If you shave there, it'll just grow in thicker!"

This advice is like a Zen koan: it simultaneously means two things at once. To a twelve-year-old boy, it's the best possible news: the sooner he starts shaving his chin, the sooner he might actually get more than just peach fuzz up there. But to a girl the same age, the advice is a cautionary tale: Don't shave your legs, et cetera! *The hair just keeps coming!*

But no matter whether you're encouraging your teen or scaring her, you can retire this old saw: shaving doesn't make hair grow in thicker, darker, or faster, or, in fact, change its growth in any way at all. Think about it; this makes sense. Your hair is made up of dead cells. The follicle, the organ that produces hair, is located a millimeter or two *below* the skin surface and has no idea what's going on up above it, any more than your feet know if you're wearing a hat.

This myth has been disproved by research as far back as 1923, when Mildred Trotter, at Washington University in Saint Louis, had three female subjects shave their body hair at different intervals for eight months. In 1928, Trotter repeated the experiment on the faces of four men, and both experiments had the same result: "Microscopic examination revealed that there was absolutely no increase in the diameter or color of the hairs before or after the shaving period." Subsequent research has borne out these findings time and time again.

Why has the myth been so persistent then? Most dermatologists blame the texture difference between shaved and unshaved hair. Longer hairs bend and flow better than little stubbly ones—in his *The Hair Book*, Philip Kingsley urges us to compare a long, flexible stalk of bamboo to a shorter, less bendy one. Hair also tends to taper, so a strand's blunter end when freshly shaven may make it feel temporarily coarser. And the idea that shaving makes your hair darker is silly: if that were true, every blond man in America would have a brunette beard by now. If you think your hair is darker after a shave, you're just getting a better look at the contrast between the hair and the (probably lighter) skin around it.

Parents: let the kids have their shaving fun! It's the only time in their lives they're going to be excited by the wearying necessity of regularly attacking their own chin/legs/pits with a sharp blade. They won't spend the rest of their lives regretting teenage shaving. They'll be too busy regretting everything else they did/said/wore as teenagers.

FALSE.

"Chocolate's making your skin break out!"

I'm turning thirty-eight the same month I'm writing these words, which presumably means my face will be clearing up any day now. The causes of acne are still not well understood by scientists, even though it affects 85 percent of American teens and, one would think, would be disproportionately more likely to afflict the nerdy kids who grow up to design case-control medical studies.

It certainly seems possible that environmental factors like diet could affect skin health. A 2002 study examined hunter-gatherer societies in remote Paraguay and Papua New Guinea, and found that acne, so common in the West, is almost unheard of there. The authors attributed the difference to the healthier, low-glycemic diet of the non-westernized societies, but attempts to tease out evidence for that claim have proved elusive. The classic study in the chocolate-and-acne field was done in 1969 by three University of Pennsylvania dermatologists, who fed chocolate bars and placebo bars, respectively, to two groups of about thirty teens apiece and found no difference in acne severity afterward. But in recent years, as other results have begun to suggest a closer connection between diet and acne, the chocolate study has been challenged on several grounds. It only lasted four weeks, for example, and dietary changes might take longer than that to affect skin health. And the placebo bars in the study were designed to be comparable to chocolate in terms of fat and calories. It's possible that the study didn't prove that cocoa butter doesn't cause zits, but only proved that cocoa butter *doesn't cause any more zits than its closest substitutes.*

This is crucial because today's "chocolate bars" actually contain very little chocolate—less than 10 percent, in some cases. Most of the rest of the bar is sugar and milk solids, and a 2009 review by the Physicians Committee for Responsible Medicine makes a pretty convincing case that sugar and dairy consumption are big contributors to the rise in acne. Data from forty-seven thousand nurses in a twenty-year Harvard study suggest that not only does milk cause pimples, but that skim milk is actually *worse* for your skin than whole milk. This has led researchers to believe the culprit isn't milkfat but instead hormones in the milk. (Androgens of all kinds have long been associated with acne.)

The American Academy of Dermatology still officially maintains that diet doesn't cause acne, but their statement on the subject now allows that "the research shows that there may be an association between diet and acne" and calls for further research. In the case of chocolate, that new research may be forthcoming. A 2011 study at the University of Miami found, for the first time, that chocolate causes acne—in fact, that feeding large quantities of pure chocolate to subjects increased their pimples sixfold. In light of the new study, even the president of the American Academy of Dermatology seemed to be backing down from his organization's claim that diet doesn't matter. "What I tell patients with acne is that, for some, chocolate plays a role, and for others, it does not," he told a WebMD reporter. The Miami researchers plan to follow up with a larger-scale randomized trial, so the muddy issue of chocolate and zits may soon be as clear as Clearasil.

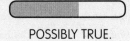

POSSIBLY TRUE.

"If you pick your zits, you'll get a brain infection and die!"

For years, beauty guides and teen magazine articles have lectured sternly about the "Danger Triangle" of the face, the region between the bridge of the nose and the corners of the mouth. Geographic triangles, you may have noticed, are always bad: the Bermuda Triangle, the Golden Triangle of the heroin trade, Baghdad's insurgent-controlled Triangle of Death. And my mom sternly warned me that my adolescent nose and mouth were also a "triangle of death": popping a zit there might lead to some kind of gross abscess that would spread back to my brain *and kill me dead.*

I thought this didn't seem plausible at all. Parents using scare tactics to keep teenagers from doing stupid things isn't exactly unheard of—hence the booming "videos of bloody decapitations" industry kept afloat by driver's ed classes. But in this case, it turns out that my mom had the medical knowledge about right. Behind the nose, blood does indeed drain through the anterior facial vein back toward the brain, so an infection there *can* occasionally spread to the sinuses, where it might cause a life-threatening blood clot called a cavernous sinus thrombosis. For many years, doctors warned that the veins in this part of the head are uniquely valveless, worsening the risk of infection, but a 2010 study showed that this was, in fact, not the case. These veins have valves like any other, but they're still the only place where the brain is this vulnerable.

But despite being technically true, the advice about popping zits is, more or less, a scare tactic, and few doctors resort to it nowadays. The medical literature on cerebral vein thrombosis reports that your odds of getting one this year are about one in three to four million, and less than 10 percent of those are the cavernous sinus thromboses that can be caused by zit popping. At one time, the condition was nearly always fatal, which may be why older generations continue to harp on it. But with modern antibiotics, the mortality rate is down to around 20 percent. It's still a life-threatening condition—and a fairly gruesome one, since symptoms can include (along with vision loss, seizures, and language disorders) bulging red eyes that make you look like a cheap Halloween mask. But your odds of dying from it are somewhere up there with shark attacks and supernovae.

Freak accidents aside, the real reason to leave pimples alone is that picking at them just makes them worse and can lead to scarring. Teens: if you don't want to look like James Woods in twenty years, leave them zits alone. But the odds are astronomically against your managing to die from popping them.

MOSTLY FALSE.

"You can't use tampons. You're a virgin!"

Girls, when you're going through that "special time" of becoming a woman, I hope you seek out advice from a knowledgeable mentor, like a mom or an older friend or a trusted seventy-four-time *Jeopardy!* champion like me. Amazingly, some girls are still being told by people who really should know better that they can't use tampons as long as they're virgins. In many cases, the implication may be that you can actually *lose your virginity* to a Tampax applicator, which is a pretty terrible thing to tell a scared girl still figuring out her first period.

I assume the problem here is an anatomical one: people visualizing the hymen as some kind of nigh-impenetrable wall, like a sheet of Saran Wrap completely covering a Georgia O'Keeffe painting. That's not true: the membrane around the vagina typically develops a ring-shaped opening about the time a fetus is born. (In rare cases of a birth defect called "imperforate hymen," the vagina may be unholey, but this condition, as a moment's thought would reveal, would make menstruation impossible, not just tampon-unfriendly, so it gets corrected surgically.) By the time a girl has her first period, she's probably had an opening in her hymen since she was a newborn, and she was clearly still a virgin back then. In fact, the condition of the hymen has little or nothing to do with virginity, contrary to popular belief. The hymen can be stretched or torn occasionally by tampon use, but it can also stretch or tear during bicycling or gymnastics or any number of other activities. At the risk of stating the obvious: not having sex is what makes you a virgin, not your bicycle seat or choice of feminine hygiene product.

Moms who worry about tampons are probably just repeating the concerns of past generations, when periods were more of a taboo subject and the convenient tampon had not yet replaced some kind of large, unwieldy panty-lining device with lots of complicated straps and buckles. (Probably. I'm just imagining here.) These older folks are still a little out of place in a world where women don't shamefully hide the realities of the menstrual cycle and actually swim, wear white pants, etc., during their periods just like the ladies in the commercials. Of course, teenage girls quickly learn that there's an upside as well to the culture's menstruation discomfort. Would it really be so easy to skip class or get out of gym if the relevant teacher was totally comfortable talking about young women's bodies and menstrual cycles? Would they rush you a hall pass just to get you out of the room before you elaborate on your "girl troubles" and actually say the word "cramps" or "period"? They might not.

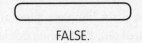

FALSE.

"If you keep touching it, you'll get hairy palms and go blind!"

Modern warnings against masturbation pale in comparison to the rhetoric of centuries past, when doctors would straight-facedly tell patients that playing with themselves could lead (to quote prominent American physician Benjamin Rush in 1830) to "vertigo, epilepsy, hypochondriasis, loss of memory, manalgia [depression], fatuity [insanity], and death." Death? These people were probably using the wrong lotion. Orson Squire Fowler, an otherwise admirable reformer for education and equal rights, thought masturbation was even worse than that:

> Pile all other evils together—drunkenness upon all cheateries, swindlings, robberies, and murders; and tobacco upon both, for it is the greater scourge; and all sickness, disease and pestilence upon all; and war as the cap sheaf of them all—and all combined does not tithe as much human deterioration and misery as does this secret sin.

To sum up: punching the munchkin is more than ten times worse than all human crime, war, and disease *put together*! Of course, Fowler was also well-known for popularizing nutty nineteenth-century fads like phrenology and octagonal houses, so maybe we shouldn't take his word for it without looking at the evidence.

There has never been any research to back the claim that masturbation causes blindness (but, as a consolation prize for "masters of their domain," it doesn't cure it either). Same goes for hairy palms, drooling, acne, physical weakness, or any other symptom from playground lore: modern medicine has been unable to link masturbation to any adverse health condition whatsoever. That didn't stop doctors in centuries past from addressing the "problem" by gruesome means: kids who masturbated sometimes had their genitals repeatedly cauterized or even excised, if that's what it took to break the habit. Most people didn't think twice about the evils-of-masturbation myth until the mid-twentieth century, when sex researchers like Alfred Kinsey and Masters and Johnson were surprised to find that the vast majority of the human race—92 percent of men and 62 percent of women—masturbates sometimes, with no resulting epidemic of blindness or anything else.

There *have* been studies, however, linking solo sex to good outcomes: lowered blood pressure, fewer menstrual problems (in women), and substantially lower risks of prostate cancer (in men). So even if the masturbation taboo isn't mutilating children's genitalia these days, it's apparently still causing cancer. Today, people who object to "self-abuse" can do so on moral or religious grounds, I guess, but they can't fall back on medical arguments. If they do, tell them they don't know jack.

FALSE.

"If you sleep on your stomach, you'll be flat-chested!"

A 2008 study by London's Sleep Assessment and Advisory Service reports that at least 7 percent of the one thousand people they tested fall asleep on their belly. (Seventy percent slept on their side, apparently the position of choice.) But I'm a little skeptical of the service's "assessment" abilities, since they gave every sleep position a cutesy name like "the Soldier" or "the Starfish" (stomach sleeping is "the Freefall") and a *lot* skeptical of their "advisory" abilities, since they claim that stomach sleeping indicates a "gregarious and brash" person who is nevertheless "nervy and thin-skinned" underneath. Okay then.

Other studies have shown that as many as 15 percent of people sleep on their stomachs. Medically speaking, it's not the ideal sleeping position—it compresses the lungs and requires sleeping with the head to one side, which isn't great for your neck and back—but it can be of special concern to tween and teenage girls, who hear from their friends, and sometimes from their moms, that they'll never get breasts if they sleep that way.

Dr. Robert Wallace, a teen advice columnist for over twenty years, has heard this question more than once, and he always answers it the same way: "Mother Nature determines your body shape, not your sleeping position." In other words, if you are genetically fated to have large breasts, no sleeping position can prevent their inexorable appearance. Ironically, girls who sleep on their stomachs have the *most* to lose in puberty, since I hear that's not the most comfortable way to sleep if you're built like Dolly Parton. "Freefallers" should probably count their blessings if they wind up a little smaller upstairs.

Just for the record, I fall asleep every night on my stomach but wake up on my back. I have no idea what the Sleep Assessment and Advisory Service would say about that, but my boobs are still nice and perky, just so you know.

FALSE.

"Alcohol kills brain cells!"

Let's be clear up front: alcohol, particularly in great quantities, has profound effects on the drinker. Some of the short-term ones (funnier friends, forgotten cares, surprise tattoos) may be great; nearly all of the long-term ones are not. Even if you're a moderate drinker who's read about the cardiovascular benefits of a glass of wine or two a day, you're still elevating other risks (accidents, injuries, even cancer) that are, statistics show, likely to outweigh the good stuff. Heavy drinkers can count on seeing damage to their liver, pancreas, and circulatory system over time. But no organ is mentioned more in parental temperance lectures than the brain, and it turns out the research on alcohol and the nervous system isn't nearly so clear-cut.

Many, many studies show a loss in brain function among longtime heavy drinkers. There's no shortage of alcoholics out there, and it's easy to design experiments that compare their cognitive performance to a sample of the general population. When researchers do these tests, they've found that alcoholics suffer from markedly higher rates of memory impairment, behavioral disorders, attention-deficit disorder, and dementia. MRI tests show that drinking does shrink the brain, though the differences are small, even in heavy drinkers (1.5 percent smaller than a normal brain, on average, and even healthy people lose 2 percent every decade just by getting older).

However, your parents' and high school teachers' insistence that "alcohol kills brain cells" has not, in general, been borne out by science. In a 1993 study in *The Lancet,* two Danish neurologists tested, for the first time, the notion that drinking alcohol would lower the number of neurons in your neocortex, the so-called "gray matter" of the brain, where reasoning happens. By counting cells in three different lobes and the hippocampus of dead brains, then extrapolating to the whole brain via the statistical magic of stereology, the scientists found that the average neocortex of both groups, heavy drinker or not, had about twenty-three billion neurons. A lifetime of alcoholism hadn't killed off brain cells at all.

There were other effects, however: the less essential "white matter" was much smaller in the brains of alcoholics, and even the cells that remained had atrophied—they were still there, but their connections weren't functioning properly. This means that the damage is reversible, says Dr. Roberta Petney, a cell biologist who specializes in chronic alcohol abuse and the brain. A dead brain cell would be dead for good, but a malfunctioning one can repair its axon or its dendrites, the structures that help it pass messages to other neurons, and get back to work. Perhaps the most feared alcoholic bogeyman for the brain is Wernicke-Korsakoff syndrome, a.k.a. "wet brain," a sudden-onset disorder that often impairs the memory and coordination of alcoholics. But research shows that the brain cell damage of Wernicke-Korsakoff syndrome is actually caused not by the alcohol itself, but by a deficiency of thiamine, a B vitamin that alcohol can inhibit. Some have suggested that "wet brain" could be eradicated altogether by including thiamine as an additive in alcoholic beverages, the same way we now add iodine to table salt.

There are lots of good reasons to keep kids away from alcohol—it's illegal, if nothing else, and you wouldn't have to spend much time on any college campus to see that young people aren't always great at moderating their drinking. But it's wrong to make them imagine that every beer they drink is permanently snuffing out neurons one by one. Almost all the effects of alcoholism on the brain can be reversed by a sustained period of abstinence or moderate drinking. And a 2005 study using data from Harvard's Nurses' Health Study showed that social drinking (about a drink a day) didn't lower cognitive test scores at all. In fact, said the authors, "a cognitive benefit from moderate alcohol intake is plausible." To paraphrase the gun lobby: Alcohol doesn't kill neurons. People kill neurons, when they lose control of their drinking.

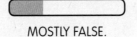

MOSTLY FALSE.

"HOW MANY TIMES DO I HAVE TO TELL YOU?"
(READER QUESTIONS)

When the hardcover edition of *Because I Said So!* was released in 2012, I unexpectedly found myself transformed in the eyes of the world from "inexplicable game show annoyance" to "omniscient parenting guru," consulted as an authority on all manner of complicated health and behavioral questions. Readers and interviewers would want me to second-guess their sainted mothers, or prop up their own parental hobbyhorses. No family secret was too personal, no childhood anecdote too bizarre. During a commercial break in one radio interview, the producer came into the studio with an urgent question. "My grandmother used to tell us not to clip our fingernails while a relative was traveling, because that would make their plane crash. Is that one really true?" she asked in dead earnest.

I told her, as straight-facedly as I could, that I knew of no study psychically linking manicures to aviation disasters. But not every question was so easy to answer. Here, as a special bonus to readers of the paperback edition, are the facts behind twelve more parental platitudes submitted by curious readers.

> "My mom always forced us to drink warm milk when we couldn't fall asleep. Does this really work?" (Colin D., Austin, Texas)

A glass of warm milk is an age-old folk remedy for insomnia. Mom's bedtime advice got a nutritional boost in the twentieth century when science discovered that milk is a good source for tryptophan, an amino acid sometimes prescribed as a sleep aid because the brain converts it into the sleep-regulating neurotransmitter melatonin.

The problem is that tryptophan doesn't work as a sleep aid unless it's taken on an empty stomach in dosages you'd never find in a glass of milk (or a serving of Thanksgiving turkey, or any of the other supposedly tryptophan-rich foods sometimes recommended by Mom's mental storehouse of 1970s-era *Reader's Digest* articles). Milk is rich in protein, and a 2003 study at MIT found that protein inhibited the effects of tryptophan on the brain. Milk protein is also a good source of tyrosine, an amino acid often found in "mental alertness" supplements for its caffeinelike properties. What's more, fully 60 percent of human adults are lactose intolerant, meaning that a bedtime glass of milk could lead to sleep-disturbing digestive problems for a majority of the world's population. For all these reasons, it's quite possible that a glass of milk before bed could perk you up instead of settle you down.

Of course, any hot beverage after Jon Stewart (or, if you're over forty-five, after Leno) will raise your body temperature and relax tense muscles. But the real reason why people swear by milk is probably psychological: the hot-milk routine soothes them, and they nod off because they think they will. But nutritionally speaking, a protein-rich snack like milk isn't the way to go before bed. Instead, try an evening meal with a high glycemic index. Your blood sugar will spike and leave you feeling sluggish hours later when it's time for bed. A big pasta dinner might not be great for your heart or your waistline, but you'll sleep like a chubby Italian baby.

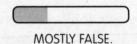

MOSTLY FALSE.

> "My dad used to make this weird whooping noise to scare us when we had the hiccups. Does that actually work? What about holding your breath or eating sugar or drinking water?"
> (Michael L., Bend, Oregon)

Those little involuntary spasms of the diaphragm that we call, adorably, "hiccups" have plagued humankind since before we came down from the trees. (Probably. I'm basing this entirely on YouTube videos I've seen of otters and porcupines and horses hiccupping.) And humans have been suggesting folk cures for them all the way back to the ancient Greeks. In Plato's *Symposium*, for example, the playwright Aristophanes gets a stubborn case of the hiccups. His doctor, Eryximachus, suggests gargling, sneezing, or—yes—just holding his breath.

These cures all work on the same principle: they briefly distract the nervous system and interfere with the respiratory system. Hiccuping is believed to be caused by a reflex arc involving the vagus nerve, a cranial nerve that tells the brain how your organs are doing. The good news is that what happens in vagus stays in vagus: if you overwhelm that nerve with *new* stimuli (the sweet taste of sugar, the concentration required to drink a glass of water upside down, the respiratory interruption of held breath or a sudden scare) you can break the cycle. Sadly, the medical literature on this point hasn't advanced much since Plato's day. There have been only a few peer-reviewed studies on hiccup cures, and all used very small, uncontrolled sample groups. One article from 1971 reported that a spoonful of granulated sugar was almost foolproof; another from 1981 had good results with a lemon wedge soaked in bitters. So there is *some* clinical evidence that, yes, sensory distraction can cure the hiccups. I also found no fewer than three studies promising to cure the hiccups with the miracle of "digital rectal massage." Yup, a finger in the butt. Now don't you think you got off easy with your dad's whooping noise?

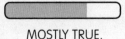

MOSTLY TRUE.

> "My mom told me that my fingernails would never digest, they would just build up in my intestines until they had to be surgically removed. The image of a giant ball of fingernails building in my colon stuck with me for a few years." (Greg W., Glendale, Arizona)

Nail-biting, which show-offy psychologists call onychophagia, certainly comes with its own small health risks, including cuticle infections and orthodontic problems. But I'll agree that those lack the dramatic flair of your mom's scare story.

As we saw on page 75, the digestive tract can get clogged if one eats too much of something indigestible. For example, hair balls ("trichobezoars," in clinical parlance) are sometimes removed from compulsive hair-eating patients. The largest one ever removed measured almost two feet long, so you can see why this illness is sometimes nicknamed "Rapunzel syndrome." But wait, you might realize at this point, fingernails are made out of keratin, the same protein as hair. If hair is indigestible, could Mom have been right? Are there fingernail bezoars as well?

There doesn't seem to be a single case of a fingernail bezoar in the medical record. (Interestingly, there are two studies of stomach bezoars composed of *actual* nails. The metal kind, like from Home Depot. People are weird.) The reason for this is probably the obvious one: we have more than one hundred thousand hairs on our head, but only ten fingers. In other words, we have plenty of hair at the ready to clog up a digestive tract, but it takes six months to regrow a new fingernail. At that rate, your gut can eliminate the clippings in the normal way. The only account I can find of fingernails in bezoars is in Echo Heron's 1988 nursing memoir *Intensive Care*, which contains the charming description of a large trichobezoar as "a hairy steak studded with fingernails." But the hair seems to have been the real problem there—the fingernails were just the nuts on the sundae, as it were.

A 2008 summary of nail-biting research by a team of Japanese and Brazilian dentists makes the claim that "stomach problems can develop" when nail-biters swallow their harvest, but their sources include no clinical evidence of this—and, frankly, I find it a little hard to believe, given the small quantities ingested. Chewing your nails may be a bad habit, but it's one your colon doesn't care about either way.

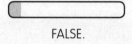

FALSE.

> "When I was little, there were days when my mother would sigh, 'I swear, I'm going to sell you to the Gypsies.' I admit that there were times I said the same to my own four darling offspring, despite never having seen a Gypsy in my life. Was this an entirely empty threat borne of a wrung-out mother's wishful thinking, or was there once a time when naughty children really were off-loaded on innocent wanderers?"
> (Katje S., Chicago, Illinois)

I'm pretty sure your mom wasn't *really* going to sell you to the Gypsies, Katje, but if she ever tried, I have some good news: the Gypsies wouldn't want you. No offense.

The myth about Gypsies buying or snatching babies was popularized by German historians of the fifteenth century, apparently on the strength of very little evidence. Many people using the "Gypsies" threat to scare unruly kids into submission were probably using the word loosely, to refer to any vaguely lawless, nomadic people. Originally, though, the literary trope of the baby-snatching Gypsy referred specifically to Europe's Romani ethnicity.

Roma people have often lived on society's fringes, and there are some kinds of crime heavily associated with so-called "Gypsies," even today. (Child pickpocket gangs of Romanian Gypsies have been widely reported by the British press, for example.) But there has never been a Gypsy kidnapping epidemic. "There is not a single well-authenticated case of kidnapping by Gypsies," wrote Irving Brown in 1924's *Gypsy Fires in America*. Brown was probably overstating things a bit, since I've found scattered news reports of Gypsy kidnapping dating back to the eighteenth century, but it seems to be (a) exceedingly uncommon and (b) directed mostly at other Gypsy clans. This makes sense. The Romani, as cultures go, are generally insular and not particularly open to outsiders. They're not sitting around the house thinking, "You know what we need up in here? *Some white babies!*"

Some scholars have guessed that the kidnapping myth may have started because Gypsies sometimes took in runaway unwed moms, or their babies. Or it might have been because Roma people are extremely heterogeneous genetically, so their non-Gyspy neighbors might have been surprised from time to time to come across Gypsy children with blond hair or blue eyes and drawn the wrong conclusion. Whatever the case, this cliché obviously has a racial angle that's a little more troublesome than scaring kids about generic strangers or bogeymen. After all, the threat of the baby-kidnapping Jew was once common as well, and sparked many an Eastern European pogrom. In our house, we avoid the race card altogether and threaten to sell the kids "on Craigslist" instead. Feel free to borrow that.

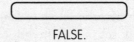

FALSE.

"If *I* can hear your earphones, it's too loud!" was what my own mother used to tell us—or at least, that's what it looked like her lips were saying. But my parents had to navigate the tricky generation gap between soup bowl–sized, spiral-corded hi-fi headphones and in-ear Walkman earphones. Did they really know what they were talking about?

Short answer: yes, even though you won't go deaf, you could lose quite a bit of hearing acuity later in life. (You already know this if you ever saw more than ten seconds of *The Osbournes*.) People often underestimate how loud their music really is. A live rock show is amplified to about 120–130 decibels, the same level as a jet taking off, and even earbud-delivered music can top 100 decibels, louder than a lawn mower. As a result, the list of veteran musicians now suffering from tinnitus and other hearing problems reads like a *Who's Who* of rock: Clapton, Townshend, Jeff Beck, Neil Young. (Highbrows don't get a pass here, by the way. A 1981 study of a Swedish orchestra found that 42 percent of classical musicians had higher-than-expected hearing loss as well.) On the other hand, Phil Collins quit touring due in part to hearing problems, so *sometimes* there's an upside.

Hearing loss in teens has risen over the past decade by 31 percent, due mostly to earphones. Brian Fligor, the head of diagnostic audiology for Children's Hospital Boston, has done a lot of work in the earbud arena and told *Time* in 2008 that a good rule of thumb is to limit iPod time: you won't damage your ears, he says, if you listen at lower than 80 percent volume for less than 90 minutes a day. The problem, he says, is people using earbuds to drown out their environment. Airplane and subway riders, for example, routinely turn their devices up higher than the 80 percent threshold. If you find yourself falling into that trap, better quality earphones may be more effective at blocking outside noise. Otherwise, teens, you're going to be spending your fifties sitting on a couch staring uncomprehendingly at your family, Ozzy-style! I bet you won't think *that's* so "cool" or "rad," will you?

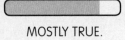

MOSTLY TRUE.

> "My mom told me I could lighten my freckles if I rubbed lemon juice on them. Any truth to that?" (Kathleen D., Val-d'Or, Quebec)

The citric acid in lemon juice is an alpha hydroxy acid, the same "AHA" touted on a $40 tube of skin cream. Alpha hydroxy acids are also used in some chemical peels, used to treat mild skin problems like freckles and acne. Among the acidic home remedies often recommended to get the same effect on the cheap: yogurt, vinegar, and, yes, lemon juice. The practice dates back at least to Cleopatra, who bathed in sour milk to give her skin that youthful, snake-ready glow.

Commercial preparations using alpha hydroxy acids have been shown to be effective in treating many skin conditions, but evidence is a little murkier for the milder concentrations used as traditional remedies. In particular, I can't see that the lemon juice–freckle combination has ever been clinically tested. But a majority of dermatologist opinions seem to favor the humble citrus fruit. "Lemon juice may fade spots if used every day," says Manhattan's dermatologist-to-the-stars Dr. Barney Kenet in his book *How to Wash Your Face*. Dr. Kenet is the hero who has pushed science to its breaking point in a valiant attempt to briefly prolong the youth of big stars like Demi Moore. He fought the good fight. I say we trust him.

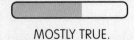

MOSTLY TRUE.

> "To this day, my mom will not use a public toilet without either (a) covering the seat with a ridiculous number of layers of toilet paper, or, in the absence of toilet paper, (b) hovering a few inches above the seat using nothing but leg muscles and sheer will. What diseases can you actually get from a public toilet seat?"
> (Chrissy J., Alexandria, Virginia)

Are we to believe the 1991 report in the *British Journal of Obstetrics and Gynaecology* to the effect that only 2 percent of all women in the United Kingdom will sit directly on a public toilet seat? Another 12 percent nested on layers of toilet paper, while a whopping 85 percent crouched above the seat in some kind of gravity-defying yoga pose! Chrissy, your mother is not alone.

As we learned on page 115, toilet seats are far from the germiest place in the house, or even in the gas station. Steering wheels, shopping carts, smartphones, kitchen faucets—all have many times the bacteria count of a typical toilet seat. In 2013, a reporter asked our friend Charles Gerba (a.k.a. Dr. Germ) if lining the toilet seat was necessary. "In my opinion, most toilet seat covers are useless," he replied. For one thing, most liners are porous enough that anything icky will seep through them anyway; for another, most diseases can't be transmitted by skin contact. Unless you have open sores on your buttocks or thighs, squatting just isn't necessary. "No one has ever acquired an STD on a toilet seat—unless they were having sex on the toilet seat!" says Abigail Salyers, former president of the American Society for Microbiology.

The famously bacteria-resistant infection MRSA is one possible exception, since it's one of the rare diseases that *can* theoretically be transmitted skin-to-skin, and it's been found on hospital toilet seats. "I suppose it's physiologically possible, but the chances of it happening are very, very slim," says Gerba. Still, that's something for the squatters to cling to—as long as they also remember to keep clinging to the towel bar or toilet paper dispenser or whatever they're using to stay safely perched up there.

Peace of mind may not be the only benefit of being a hoverer, however. An Israeli doctor studying "hoverers" in 2003 found that, in general, subjects cut their toilet time in half when they switched to squatting, and strained over the bowl considerably less. The rewards are obvious: more productive poops in less time, with lower risk of hemorrhoids. But if you're listing the health benefits of hovering, "disease prevention" is definitely a distant number 2.

MOSTLY FALSE.

"We were never allowed to get chocolate from the candy counter, but had to settle for its distant cousin carob, which we were assured was just as good. What is carob, anyway? Is it healthier than chocolate, like mom used to say?" (Emily S., Columbus, Georgia)

Chocolate is made by roasting the seeds of a South American tree. Carob is made by roasting the seed pods of an entirely unrelated Mediterranean shrub. But the end results are vaguely similar in texture and flavor, so carob can often be found in health food stores, where it's billed as a healthier substitute for chocolate.

In truth, the health benefits of carob are pretty minor. Carob doesn't contain the alkaloids caffeine or theobromine, so it won't give you the same buzz as chocolate—but on the other hand, it won't kill your pets (see page 171). Carob evangelists will always tell you that it's lower in fat than chocolate (healthier!) and higher in sugar (so you won't have to sweeten it as much—healthier!). As a moment's thought will reveal, both these arguments can't be right. In fact, both are meaningless, since both carob and chocolate need lots of extra fat *and* sugar added before you can bake a cookie with them, which cancels out any nutritional difference. And the fat added to make carob edible is often a cholesterol-raising tropical oil, so score one point for chocolate.

What about the taste? I had never actually eaten carob myself, so I decided to pick up a bag of carob chips from our local socially conscious grocery store and force my kids to participate in a taste test. It wasn't an overwhelming success.

"NO," said my ten-year-old son immediately, grimacing and looking for somewhere to spit.

"What do you mean, no?" I asked.

"It means I'm never eating another one of those again. It doesn't taste remotely like chocolate."

"What does it taste like?"

"It tastes like pickles," said my daughter. I popped a few in my mouth. She was right—they tasted like a cup of coffee percolated with pickle juice instead of water—a little salty, a little bitter. If they hadn't been cruelly disguised as chocolate chips, I don't know if I could have picked out chocolate as the thing they were trying to be.

"What would you do if Mom and I made a batch of cookies with the rest of these?"

"I would throw it away and say, 'Please give me another one without fake chocolate chips in it.'"

We gave the rest to the dog.

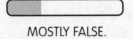

MOSTLY FALSE.

> "Can you really get lice from trying on other people's hats, the way moms and teachers always say?" (Brian A., Auburn, Maine)

Head lice are, in a way, the ultimate parental fear. It takes our usual neuroses—you'll send a child to school and he or she will come home with a split lip, or a bad grade, or knowing the word "douchebag"—and amps them up to science-fiction proportions. Suddenly, it's possible to send beautiful, innocent children to kindergarten and have them come home *literally crawling with bloodsucking parasites and their eggs*—an *Alien* movie going on in miniature inches above their eyebrows.

Head lice are actually a fairly common malady, affecting 10 to 20 percent of elementary school students worldwide—that's as many as 12 million infestations in the United States every year. Transmission has nothing to do with health or hygiene. Head-to-head contact with one louse-y person is all it takes. With this in mind, many parents take drastic measures, like banning kids from touching anything that may have touched another kid's head, whether it's a hat or a comb or a pillowcase at a sleepover. "You can ask your child not to share hats, scarves, combs, brushes, hair decorations, and other personal belongings," says the Mayo Clinic, while allowing that this may not be a realistic goal.

You think? More to the point, it's ineffective. Dermatologists studying head lice have found evidence of indirect transmission (that is, via inanimate objects) to be somewhere between negligible and nonexistent. A 2000 study of four Australian primary schools collected 5,500 lice from students' heads . . . but not a single one from their head*wear*, even though more than 1,000 hats were carefully examined. This isn't too surprising, given that a head louse's teeny-tiny claws are terrific at gripping a shaft of hair but pretty useless for anything else (in particular, smooth, hard surfaces like headbands and sports helmets are almost completely louse-proof) and that lice start to die about nine hours after being dislodged from a delicious, blood-filled scalp. I found only one experimental study that was able to successfully transmit lice via cloth, and it didn't use real hats or real heads.

The Centers for Disease Control allows that "spread by contact with inanimate objects and personal belongings may occur but is very uncommon." Given the kind of full-body roughhousing that goes on between nine-year-olds at playgrounds and playdates, I don't think the dreaded Swapped Baseball Cap is a louse vector that parents need to tear their hair out over.

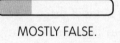

MOSTLY FALSE.

> "Mom and Dad would always warn us that playing with fire would cause us to pee in the bed that night. Never stopped us from playing with fire. We never peed in the bed. Well, except for my little brother, but he always did. Ever heard of this one?"
> (Angela J., San Antonio, Texas)

U.S. fire departments get called 56,300 times every year because dumb kids were playing with matches or a lighter. These fires cause, on average, 110 annual deaths and more than $286 million in property damage. If little white lies have *any* place in parenthood, pyromania would seem to be a good reason to deploy them.

But the lecture about fire-playing causing bed-wetting isn't just a smoke screen. It appears to have started in centuries past as a sincere belief. In 1914, *The Journal of the American Medical Association* listed it among the "curious superstitions (from) a less-enlightened age" commonly found among patients—even "people of some education and otherwise fairly intelligent." I've found more recent citations of this old wives' tale coming from a veritable United Nations of moms: British, Scandinavian, Latin American, Korean, Japanese. Because of its fire/water dichotomy, folklorists connect it to other beliefs in which a treatment causes or cures its opposite—taking hot drinks for a cold, for example.

No less a luminary than Sigmund Freud seems to have taken the belief at face value. In a classic case study from his 1899 *The Interpretation of Dreams,* he learns that his patient "Dora" has recurring dreams of a house fire, and he connects the fear of fire to her childhood bedwetting. Dora has never heard of the matches thing and supposes that it's just a safety issue, but Freud insists that parents who deploy this warning are genuinely worried about their kids becoming bed-wetters! "Perhaps it is believed that (people) will dream of fire and then try to put it out with water," he guesses. "I cannot say exactly."

Subsequent psychologists ran with Freud's theory, and for a time, childhood pyromania and enuresis (bed-wetting), along with animal cruelty, were the three legs of the "Macdonald triad" for predicting serial killers! The enuresis link to criminal behavior has since been discredited, but it seems the association remains for lots of superstitious parents. Moms and dads: there are lots of ways to discourage your little junior arsonists without giving them a complex about wetting the bed as well. Who knows? If they're ever playing with fire *in bed*, bed-wetting may actually save the day.

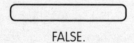

FALSE.

"My dad would yell at us if we got too close to a dead squirrel, telling us we would catch a disease from it. Is that true?"
(Ron T., Highlands Ranch, Colorado)

Without seeing the carcass in question, Ron, I can't be 100 percent sure, of course. But in general, yes, your parents were right to keep you away from the late Mr. Squirrel. Roadkill isn't one of those things that *sound* gross but are actually awesome, like childbirth, or chocolate-covered bacon. Roadkill's disgusting reputation is entirely deserved.

It's true that the bacteria at work in a decomposing bird or possum aren't pathogenic. But the real problem is what killed the animal in the first place. What if it was West Nile? What if—despite the tire tread that was clearly the cause of death—the poor guy also had rabies? Both diseases are deadly serious and continue to be contagious after death. In 2012, a young girl camping in your home state of Colorado tried to bury a dead squirrel and almost died from a subsequent attack of bubonic plague (!), the state's first case in years. Her parents said she never even touched the squirrel, but plague-carrying fleas evidently made the jump onto her jacket. Presto: possible medieval epidemic in Denver. So tell your tender-hearted little kids not to bury dead animals and your mean ones not to poke them with sticks. The Circle of Life will take care of all of that for them. Mostly the maggot and coyote parts of the Circle.

TRUE.

"My mom always told us to sing the ABCs in our heads while washing our hands. Does washing for that long actually make our hands clean enough?"
(David E., Hartsdale, New York)

As mentioned on page 117, an effective hand-washing takes about twenty seconds of vigorous scrubbing—any less and you might leave little germy things stuck between crannies and clinging to fingernails. Is the familiar alphabet song (probably an invention of Boston schoolmasters in the 1830s, based on the same French folk song we also sing as "Twinkle, Twinkle, Little Star" and "Baa, Baa, Black Sheep") a reliable pre-K proxy for a twenty-second stopwatch? I enlisted my kids to find out.

When I asked them to sing the alphabet song for me, the results were fine: their renditions took between twenty-two and twenty-five seconds. But when I told them they had to wash their hands for the duration of the song, both kids happened on the same solution: motoring through the twenty-six letters as fast as they could, like the fast-talking guy in those old Federal Express ads. This approach led to as little as five seconds of hand-washing in some cases.

So the timing of the ABCs is about right, as long it's supervised to make sure kids don't try to game the system. You might also want to be sure the twenty seconds is spent actively rubbing the hands together, scrubbing between fingers, targeting the nails, etc., instead of in the dreamy reverie that often afflicts my kids above a bathroom sink.

In 2009, National Public Radio wondered if there was a better twenty-second selection for *adult* hand-washers to hum. After all, many lives have undoubtedly been saved by the American Heart Association's recent recommendation that CPR be performed to the rhythm of the Bee Gees' "Stayin' Alive." Among the hygienic hits suggested for the aging boomers who listen to public radio: the chorus of "Sweet Caroline" (twenty-three seconds), the guitar-riff intro to "Layla" (twenty-five seconds), and the multitracked bridge of "Bohemian Rhapsody" (over a minute!). The Queen song won their listener poll, despite not being particularly close to the correct length. I'm not sure if they even counted my write-in vote for the obvious choice: the *Jeopardy!* "think" music.

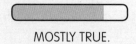

MOSTLY TRUE.

Acknowledgments

Obviously, I'm not the first person to try to make a buck scrutinizing and debunking popular myths. I've loved this sort of thing ever since I was ten years old, reading Jan Harold Brunvand's meticulous research into urban legends and Tom Burnam's wonderful pair of *Misinformation* dictionaries. But I'm especially indebted to my three idols in the field of conventional-wisdom deflating, who were huge influences on this book: columnist "Cecil Adams," of "The Straight Dope" fame; Barbara and David Mikkelson, who run the urban legend reference Snopes.com; and TV's valiant *MythBusters*. Truly they are the Father, Son, and Holy Ghost of the genre.

Most of my sources for this book were primary research in scientific and medical journals, but I had a lot of help finding them. The Ig Nobel Prizes, awarded every year by *Annals of Improbable Research* magazine for goofy scientific discoveries, are a treasure trove for this kind of thing. Also especially helpful were *The New York Times'* weekly "Really?" column and two collections of medical myths by Dr. Aaron Carroll and Dr. Rachel Vreeman: *Don't Swallow Your Gum!* and *Don't Cross Your Eyes . . . They'll Get Stuck That Way!* And never, ever try to estimate childhood dangers without checking the National Electronic Injury Surveillance System. That would be more ill-advised than running with scissors on an escalator with a plastic bag over your head.

A few of the entries in this book were previously published, in modified form, in my weekly "Debunker" column for the indispensable deal-of-the-day website Woot.com, which I heartily recommend. They also own a gigantic Styrofoam carving of my head. True story.

Thanks to my agent, Jud Laghi, and to Brant Rumble, who sounds like a superhero or wrestler but is actually my editor at Scribner. He made every part of this book better except for the title, which stumped both of us, so we held a contest. The winning entry, *Because I Said So!*, was first suggested by one Philip Romano and saved our bacon.

My sincerest thanks to all the friends who scoured their memories for dubious bits of parental wisdom—and, by extension, their dubious parents, living or dead! I also asked my virtual friends on the social news website Reddit.com for suggestions—and got thousands of them. This being the Internet, I also got a few angry "Why should we do your homework for you, *Jeopardy!* douche? Write your own damn book!" replies, and dozens of bacon jokes. But among the Reddit suggestions were twenty-odd parental clichés I hadn't thought of and that ended up making the final cut, so I promised to thank people named (or "named," in some cases) blitzcreeg10, Chris Cosler, Josh Damoulakis, Benjamin Dixon, dungeye, Jenna Gardner, Caitlin Hakala, Jenna Klaft, Justin Lefler, Matt Ludwig, Kevin Mayer, Christina Maynard, MoJ0_jojo, Noah from Chicago, Annika Piiroinen, pimanrules, Red-Dorf, TheDogKing, TheMagicHorsey, Philip M. Thompson, Terry Tourangeau, Twiek, wheresmyhou, Bruce Sterling "sirbruce" Woodcock, and Arthur Z. Redditors: as godless, libertarian-leaning smart-asses go, you are the best!

Finally, my undying gratitude to my own parents, who (a) raised me with a burning desire to figure out the difference between conventional wisdom and actual scientific fact, and (b) still gave me lots of crazy but well-meaning advice that I finally got to debunk in these pages. Without both parts, this book never would have happened. Or at least it would have been much shorter, had a different cover and title, and been a series of erotic vignettes about vampires who solve murders. Thanks, Mom and Dad! I'm coming by later with my laundry.

Ken Jennings
May 2012